DISCARDED BY
MEMPHIS PUBLIC LIBRARY

Herbert Hoover

and the

Historians

Also published by the Hoover Presidential Library Association

The Problems of Lasting Peace Revisited
A Scholarly Conference (1986)
THOMAS T. THALKEN, ED.

Doors of Opportunity
The Life and Legacy of Herbert Hoover (1988)
FRANK T. NYE, JR.

American Individualism (1922) and
The Challenge to Liberty (1934);
reissued in one volume (1989)
HERBERT HOOVER

HERBERT HOOVER and the HISTORIANS

Essays by
Ellis W. Hawley
Patrick G. O'Brien
Philip T. Rosen
Alexander DeConde

Introduction by
Tom Walsh

Edited by
Mark M. Dodge

Herbert Hoover Presidential Library Association, Inc.
West Branch, Iowa

©1989 by the Herbert Hoover Presidential Library Association, Inc.

All Rights Reserved. No part of this publication may be reproduced, stored in a retrieval system, or transmitted, in any form or by means electronic, mechanical, photocopying, recording, or otherwise, except for the inclusion of brief quotations in a review, without prior permission in writing from the publishers.

Library of Congress Cataloging-in-Publication Data

Herbert Hoover and the Historians

   Bibliography: p.
   1. United States--Politics and government--1929-1933--Historiography. 2.United States--Foreign relations--1929-1933--Historiography. 3. Hoover, Herbert Clark, 1874-1964. I. Hawley, Ellis Wayne, 1929-   . II. Dodge, Mark M.
E801.H47 1989   973.91'6'072   88-35795

ISBN 0-938469-03-7
ISBN 0-938469-02-9 (pbk.)

Paperback cover illustration by J. N. "Ding" Darling

Herbert Hoover Presidential Library Association, Inc.
P.O. Box 696
West Branch, Iowa 52358

Manufactured in the United States of America.

Contents

Introduction
  Tom Walsh / vii

Herbert Hoover and Modern American History: Sixty Years After / 1
  Ellis W. Hawley

Hoover and the Historians: The Reconstruction of a President / 39
  Patrick G. O'Brien
  Philip T. Rosen

Herbert Hoover and Foreign Policy: A Retrospective Assessment / 87
  Alexander DeConde

Herbert Hoover: A Selected Bibliography / 117
  Richard Dean Burns
  Autobiographies, Biographies & Memoirs / 117
    Biographies / 117
    Philosophy / 119
    Historiography / 121
    Speeches and Writing / 121
  Hoover's Political Life / 121
    General / 121
    The Early Years / 121
    World War I and Aftermath / 122
      Food Administrator / 123
      Relief / 124

Secretary of Commerce / 125
    Books & Dissertations / 125
    Essays / 125
The Postpresidential Years / 126
    As New Deal Critic / 127
    As Foreign Policy Critic / 127
The Hoover Commisions (1948/1955) / 127
The Hoover Presidency / 128
    Overviews / 128
        Books / 128
        Essays / 129
    Administration & Politics / 129
        Books / 129
        Essays / 130
    Agriculture & Conservation / 132
    Business, Trade & Transportation / 133
    Finance & Labor / 133
    The Depression (Causes & Reactions) / 133
        A Prelude to the New Deal? / 134
        Social Reform / 135
        Minorities / 135
    Evaluation / 136
    "Smear Books" / 137
Hoover and Foreign Affairs / 138
    General / 138
        Books / 138
        Essays / 138
    East Asia / 139
    Europe / 139
    Western Hemisphere / 140
    International Economic & Politics / 140
    Naval Limitations & Disarmament / 140

Introduction

Pulitzer Prize winning cartoonist J.N. "Ding" Darling's 1929 portrayal of over-achiever Herbert Hoover on the following page best explains why this volume is both necessary and useful. Ever since 1914, when Herbert Hoover took his first steps on "the slippery road of public of public life," writers from tabloid journalists to distinguished historical scholars have wrestled with the same basic question: Who *is* Herbert Hoover?

Now, 75 years later, that same question confronts the latest wave of researchers to reach the reading rooms of the Hoover Presidential Library in West Branch, Iowa; the Hoover Institution on War, Revolution and Peace in Palo Alto, California; the National Archives in Washington, D.C.; and of archival libraries throughout a world indelibly stamped by this globe-trotting figure, whose 90 remarkable years encompassed many lives. Mining engineer, humanitarian, politician and elder statesman: few public figures have had greater impact on the turbulent 20th Century.

As a road map for those just beginning their search for the *real* Herbert Hoover—or as a traveller's aid to those who feel lost along the way—this volume is offered with our best wishes for an intellectually rewarding journey. The three review essays brought together here are revised and updated versions of earlier research by Ellis Hawley, Patrick O'Brien and Philip Rosen, and Alexander DeConde. The original Hawley essay—"Herbert Hoover and Modern American

How Will Hoover Go Down in History? [1929]

History: Fifty Years After"—was among those selected for inclusion in *Herbert Hoover Reassessed*, a Congressional tribute to Hoover compiled by a life-long admirer, U.S. Senator Mark O. Hatfield. The O'Brien-Rosen collaboration first appeared in the summer and fall of 1981, as a two-part article published by Iowa's State Historical Society in *The Annals of Iowa* under the title "Hoover and the Historians: The Resurrection of a President." O'Brien subsequently updated the 1981 version in an essay published in the *Annals* in 1988. The DeConde contribution was originally published in 1981 by the United States Senate to commemorate the fiftieth anniversary of Hoover's inauguration.

These new versions, in combination with Professor Richard Dean Burns extensive Hoover bibliography, will enable any Hoover explorer to chart a course of further study. Be forewarned, however, that both casual observers and serious historians encounter unexpected twists on such voyages. In dealing with a man as complex and issues as diverse as those holding Hoover's attention throughout his long life, it seems that the more you learn, the more that there is to learn. Like landscape artists, each putting brush to canvas to depict the mountain from their own unique perspective, historians find many Hoovers. To paraphrase Ellis Hawley, the controversy over Hoover's place in modern history is far from over. Instead, it continues to evolve through new phases of conflicting evidence and competing perspectives.

The recent opening of First Lady Lou Henry Hoover's revealing personal papers, the emergence of George H. Nash's definitive multi-volume Hoover biography series and the diminution of the generational vilification of the man Mark Hatfield describes as "modern history's most underrated and misunderstood president" have prompted new interest in Hoover. Requests to the Hoover Presidential Library Association for research fellowships and grants have hit record levels. It's an exciting state of affairs for those of us who know that the explorers of the past have only glimpsed beneath the surface of a man whose depths may require a team of scholastic Cousteaus. It is our hope that this volume provides you with the charts you'll need. Those of us moored on the sea of Iowa prairie grass that surrounds the Hoover birthplace cottage wish you Godspeed.

Tom Walsh
Executive Director
Hoover Presidential Library Association
West Branch, Iowa

Herbert Hoover and Modern American History: Sixty Years After

Ellis W. Hawley

> This is a revised and enlarged version of the essay that originally appeared in *Herbert Hoover Reassessed: Essays Commemorating the Fiftieth Anniversary of the Inauguration of Our Thirty-First President.* Senate Document No. 96-63. 96th Congress, 2nd Session. Washington, DC: GPO, 1981.

Sixty years ago, as Herbert Hoover assumed the duties of the presidency, few historians would have argued that history was passing him by. On the contrary, he seemed to be at the very center of modern American development. In an age of engineering and administration, he had become the great practitioner of these arts. In a world being modernized by American expertise and capital, he had been a pioneering figure. And in a society that had allegedly moved beyond regulatory formulas and was developing responsible self-government in its economic sphere,[1] he had been in the vanguard of the movement. If ever a president had embodied modern tendencies, the man being inaugurated in 1929 seemed to do so.

Four years later, as a defeated Hoover left office, few historians were inclined to defend the views that had been so widely held in 1929. The notion that he had been on the cutting edges of modern history was now being dismissed as reactionary propaganda. His reputation as an organizational genius and builder of economic self-government had been

---

[1] See James C. Malin, *The United States after the World War* (New York: Ginn, 1930), 535-543.

shattered. And his career, far from entitling him to a place among innovators and progressives, was now perceived as a long exercise in disguising reactionary aims, blocking the kind of government appropriate for a twentieth-century democracy, and blaming others for his deficiencies and failures. By this time, moreover, Hoover's own defense tended to stress his role as a conserver rather than an innovator. In his battles against statist proposals, he was now depicting himself less as a builder of a new managerial society and more as the preserver of traditional freedoms, values, and wisdoms. To an altered constituency he was becoming the great individualist and libertarian rather than the great manager and social engineer.

In these three perspectives, each articulated between 1929 and 1933, one can find the seeds of a continuing controversy concerning Hoover's place in modern history. Subsequent biographical and historical writings tended to delineate not one but three Hoovers and current scholarship has sought to shed light on which of these delineations, if any, corresponded to historical reality. A survey of the controversy may help to put such scholarship in perspective. It should at least help to clarify the shifting frameworks behind differing historical judgements. And it is with these ends in mind that I propose to explore the divergent modes of perceiving America's thirty-first president as these have operated and interacted over the past six decades.

I

In the quarter century after 1933, writing about Hoover was dominated by the perspective of his depression critics. Most historians, as Arthur Schlesinger has noted,[2] portrayed him as a dour, complacent, and reactionary figure, mentally frozen in the past, unable to grasp the problems of his age,

---

[2] Arthur Schlesinger, Jr., "Hoover Makes a Comeback," *New York Review of Books*, 8 March 1979, 10.

and determinedly sacrificing human welfare on the altar of an outmoded antistatism. In no way was he considered either a true modernizer or a true defender of what was worth saving in the national heritage. Such views, however, did not go entirely unchallenged. Competing perceptions were also articulated. And as Albert Romansco noted in an essay published in 1974,[3] these produced two groups of writings in which Hoover appeared as a much more positive figure. In Romasco's terminology, there was not only the Hoover of "liberal" history but the ones depicted in a "conservative" rival and in a "deviant revisionism."

Of these competing perspectives, the first was largely an extension of the defense that Hoover and his supporters had developed in 1931 and 1932. This had articulated a view of history in which Hooverian activities had been conservative or restorative. They had been directed not toward building a new order but toward strengthening the traditional one against domestic subversives, foreign malignancies, and fair-weather patriots. Such had been the burden of Hoover's campaign addresses, and such was the view that continued to be articulated in a "conservative" literature deploring the post-1933 innovations and arguing that they had been neither necessary nor socially desirable. In the 1930s it appeared in the histories of the administration written by such former Hoover associates as Ray Lyman Wilbur, Arthur M. Hyde, Walter H. Newton, and William Starr Myers.[4] In the 1940s it found expression in Eugene Lyons' *Our Unknown Ex-President* and John T. Flynn's *The Roosevelt Myth*.[5] And in

---

[3]Albert U. Romasco, "The End of the Old Order or the Beginning of the New," in Martin Fausold and George Mazuzan, eds., *The Hoover Presidency: A Reappraisal* (Albany: State University of New York Press, 1974), 69-86.

[4]Ray Lyman Wilbur and Arthur M. Hyde, *The Hoover Policies* (New York: Scribner's, 1937); William Starr Myers and Walter H. Newton, *The Hoover Administration* (New York: Scribner's, 1936).

[5]Eugene Lyons, *Our Unknown Ex-President: A Portrait of Herbert Hoover* (Garden City, NY: Doubleday, 1948).

the 1950s it was reiterated in Hoover's *Memoirs* and in Edgar Eugene Robinson's study of the Roosevelt presidency.[6]

More specifically, such writings tended to depict Hoover not as a great socio-economic organizer but as a dedicated defender of free-enterprise and local initiative as they had developed in the American setting. They said little about his faith in government-induced organizational action as a solution for economic and social problems, much of his warnings concerning unwise governmental policies and the evils of statist regulation and federal doles. They viewed the depression, moreover, not as a product of Hooverian policy but as the result of economic dislocations set in train by the First World War. And they saw Hoover's leadership after 1929 not as a failure but as a major factor in parrying the blows from abroad, neutralizing adverse political developments at home, and thus preserving a system that could have brought renewed growth and prosperity had not the New Deal intervened. Politically, to be sure, Hoover had failed in his efforts to retain power. But this was attributed to popular impatience heightened by slanderous and irresponsible misrepresentation. It was not the failure of responsible leadership. Nor was it a reason for accepting the subsequent decline into statist regimentation. For those able to see clearly, Hoover had shown that economic recovery could be secured without compromising the integrity and viability of a truly liberal system.

For Hooverian loyalists these writings provided reassurance, and for those seeking to roll back the New Deal they provided arguments against its necessity and Americanism. But as history they were marred by unabashed partisanship, questionable documentation, and uncritical endorsement of conservative political beliefs. They could be dismissed as exercises in political polemic or defensive

---

[6]Herbert C. Hoover, *The Memoirs of Herbert Hoover*, 3 vols. (New York: MacMillan, 1951); Edgar Eugene Robinson, *The Roosevelt Leadership, 1933-1945* (Philadelphia: Lippincott, 1955).

apologetics, offering a version of the past that serious students of the subject could safely ignore. And in scholarly circles they were so dismissed. They produced no scholarly debates of the sort that stimulate detailed historical study. Nor did they alter in any substantial way the intellectual framework shaping scholarly inquiry, textbook writing, and class-room teaching.

The reigning assumptions of this framework continued to hold that modern America had taken shape during its reform presidencies, especially those of Theodore Roosevelt, Woodrow Wilson, and Franklin D. Roosevelt. The periods between them had been barren, frivolous, or reactionary interludes, deserving and receiving little historical study. And in the absence of such study, the anti-Hoover rhetoric of 1932 and 1933 continued to be accepted as historical reality. Among scholars, to be sure, the outright "hate" and "smear" literature[7] was early recognized as containing gross distortions and sheer fabrications. But essentially, Hoover remained an anti-Roosevelt. His activities served as backdrops or foils for the progressive innovations of the New Deal, and his accepted interpreters were historians primarily concerned with tracing, explaining, and celebrating the "Roosevelt Revolution." His role in modern history, at least for most scholars and students, was the one depicted in such works as Basil Rauch's *History of the New Deal*, Dixon Wecter's *The Age of the Great Depression*, Mario Einaudi's *The Roosevelt Revolution*, and Arthur Schlesinger's *Crisis of the Old Order*.[8]

[7]Books, for example, like Walter Liggett, *The Rise of Herbert Hoover* (New York: Fly, 1932); John Hamill, *The Strange Career of Mr. Hoover Under Two Flags* (New York: Faro, 1931); and James O'Brien, *Hoover's Millions and How He Made Them* (New York: O'Brien, 1932).

[8]Basil Rauch, *The History of the New Deal, 1933-1938* (New York: Creative Age, 1944); Dixon Wecter, *The Age of the Great Depression 1929-1941* (New York: Macmillan, 1948); Mario Einaudi, *The Roosevelt Revolution* (New York: Harcourt, Brace, 1959); Arthur

For such interpreters the great tragedy of the early 1930s was that the innovations associated with Franklin D. Roosevelt and the New Deal had been so slow in coming. These were what the country had needed if it was to have a humane society and a viable economic order. Only social reactionaries and prisoners of outmoded ideological systems and symbols could have believed otherwise. And having thus identified the villains in the story, such accounts had no hesitation about placing Hoover among them. He had failed, so they charged, to devise realistic recovery and reform programs, had worked instead to thwart and discredit those who proposed them, and had continued, in the face of overwhelming evidence to the contrary, to proclaim that prosperity was "just around the corner" and that traditional welfare institutions were performing well. His presidency had cost the nation a great deal, both in individual suffering and social travail; and had he been more skilled in the political arts, it could have done even more damage. If the citizenry had anything for which to be thankful, it was the political ineptitude that destroyed Hoover's standing as a leader and facilitated a shift of power to those capable of acting humanely and realistically.

On the question of whether Hoover should be celebrated or castigated, mainstream history reached conclusions diametrically opposed to those appearing in the conservative writings. Yet on two matters the liberal and conservative interpretations did tend to agree. Both viewed Hoover as a defender of classic individualism, and both saw his policies and ideas as being polar opposites from those embraced by Franklin D. Roosevelt and the New Deal. This was an agreement also shared by revisionists who were reinterpreting and becoming more critical of Roosevelt's leadership. In *The American Political Tradition*, Richard Hofstadter stressed Roosevelt's opportunism and his lack of either depth or

Schlesinger, Jr., *The Crisis of the Old Order, 1919-1933* (Boston: Houghton Mifflin, 1957).

direction.[9] But Hoover, as depicted in the same work, remained the last presidential spokesman for an unmanaged capitalist economy and for the once hallowed doctrine of laissez-faire individualism.

Still, even in this period, the agreement on these two matters was never unanimous. A deviant revisionism also appeared, rejecting the kinds of political rhetoric that mainstream and conservative writers credited, and arguing that the New Deal, far from being a polar opposite of Hooverism, was essentially an extension and elaboration of what Hoover had started. Writing in *The Yale Review* in 1935, Walter Lippman[10] developed the idea of a Hoover-Roosevelt continuum, noting in particular how Hoover's programs had anticipated the New Deal actions and arguing strongly that the great divide in national policy had come in 1929 and 1930 rather than 1933. Twelve years later the historian Broadus Mitchell[11] depicted Hoover and Roosevelt not as opposites but as proponents of differing forms of state capitalism, neither of them successful in restoring prosperity or correcting the basic defects in the American economic order. And writing in the early 1950s, Eric Goldman[12] concluded that much of the New Deal had emerged from the

---

[9]Richard Hofstadter, *The American Political Tradition and the Men Who Made It* (New York: Knopf, 1948), 281-314. The few scholarly articles of the period were also inclined to accept the perspectives associated with Hoover's critics and rivals. See, for example, Gerald D. Nash, "Herbert Hoover and the Origins of the Reconstruction Finance Corporation," *Mississippi Valley Historical Review* 46 (December 1959), 455-468; and James H. Shideler, "Herbert Hoover and the Federal Farm Board Project,"*Mississippi Valley Historical Review* 42 (March 1956), 710-729.

[10]Walter Lippmann, "The Permanent New Deal," *Yale Review* 24 (June 1935), 649-667.

[11]Broadus Mitchell, *Depression Decade* (New York: Holt, Rinehart, 1947).

[12]Eric Goldman, *Rendezvous with Destiny* (New York: Knopf, 1952), 306-373.

development of "associational activities" between 1912 and 1932. This had been a form of progressivism, and with it Hoover had been clearly and closely linked.

Also contributing to this deviant revisionism was the historian William Appleman Williams. Writing in the mid-1950s,[13] he emphasized the corporative designs that had shaped public policy during the Republican era as well as the New Deal. The former had not been an era of isolationism and laissez-faire. Nor had Hoover been a champion and defender of such philosophies. On the contrary, as Williams viewed him, he had been a sophisticated analyst of modern capitalism's contradictions and dangers, recognizing both the need for new communitarian structures and the evils that could flow from using statist power as a substitute for community action. In both respects, Williams argued, Hoover had been far more perceptive than Roosevelt; and unlike earlier revisionists, Williams saw the New Deal not as an improvement on Hoover's innovations but as a perversion and corruption of them along lines that Hoover had foreseen and warned against.[14]

Initially, however, neither Williams nor the other revisionists had much impact on the study and interpretation of Hoover's ideas, policies, and activities. Through most of the 1950s the framework that they were challenging remained firmly established. It continued, as in the 1940s, to block serious consideration and testing of rival views, and under these circumstances accounts of Hoover's presidency and public career continued to serve as foils for or backdrops to the New Deal. It was not until the established framework began to crumble, primarily as a result of challenges from

[13] William Appleman Williams, "The Legend of Isolationism in the 1920s," *Science and Society* 18 (Winter 1954), 1-20; Williams, "Right Crisis: Wrong Order," *Nation* 84 (March 23, 1957), 257-260.

[14] The argument would be more fully developed in William Appleman Williams, *The Tragedy of American Diplomacy* (Cleveland: World, 1959).

other quarters, that these revisionist perspectives helped to bring a general reconsideration of Hoover's role in modern American. history.

II

The kind of challenges capable of weakening accepted views were slow in coming. But by the late 1950s several developments had set the stage for their appearance. One was simply the cooling of earlier political passions, partly as a matter of time, partly because they could not be fully transmitted to a new and younger generation of historical scholars. A second was the growing awareness of consensual factors and basic continuities in American history, an awareness heightened perhaps by the international situation and new social pressures for national unity. A third was the discovery of historical phenomena difficult to fit into the established framework; and a fourth, or more accurately a part of the third, was the application to history of new insights being generated in the social sciences, especially in the disciplines of sociology, political science, institutional economics, and management studies. Each of these developments facilitated a rethinking of America's past, and by the end of the decade several kinds of revisionism were producing heated scholarly debates and a new interest in long neglected subjects and periods.

One such challenge to established perceptions came from historians emphasizing the extent to which Americans had always shared common values and maintained a national consensus.[15] The central story of the American past, as they told it, was not one of conflict and discontinuity. It was a story rather of persisting dedication to the principles of Lockean liberalism; a story in which reform had consisted

[15]The most influential work was Louis Hartz, *The Intellectual Tradition in America* (New York: Harcourt, Brace, 1955). Also influential were the historians Daniel Boorstin and Clinton Rossiter.

chiefly of measures through which this uniquely American system had adapted itself to meet modern needs; and hence a story of apparent antagonists actually engaged in a common enterprise of nation building. The search now was for continuities and shared values that the older history had obscured, and one result was a growing disposition to question the accepted wisdom about Hoover-Roosevelt dichotomies and New Deal innovation.

A second challenge to accepted historical wisdom came from historians strongly influenced by the work being done in the social sciences.[16] Modern America, they were now suggesting, had been shaped less by democratic forces and reform presidencies than by status drives, interest-group interaction, managerial impulses, and urbanizing processes. Its central story, like that of the other twentieth-century societies, had been one of traditional ordering mechanisms giving way to more modern, more rational, more technocratic ones, all to the accompaniment of numerous disorders, social strains, and cultural conflicts. And while some still saw the Wilsonians and the New Dealers as the great modernizers, rationalizers, and mobilizers, the new framework also opened the door for another look at the organizational visions and activities of the Harding, Coolidge, and Hoover years.

A third such challenge, appearing to some extent as a response to the first two, was that coming from historians who were now broadening their definitions of "progressive" and recognizing greater degrees of continuity, consensus, and non-economic motivation. As told by them, the central story of modern America was still one of reformist impulses moving the nation onward and upward toward the realization

---

[16]Among the major works reflecting and helping to shape this perspective were Richard Hofstadter, *The Age of Reform* (New York: Knopf, 1955); Samuel P. Hays, *The Response to Industrialism* (Chicago: University of Chicago Press, 1957); Robert H. Wiebe, *Businessmen and Reform* (Cambridge: Harvard University Press, 1962); and Alfred D. Chandler, *Strategy and Structure* (Cambridge: Harvard University Press, 1962).

of greater democracy. But the range of those seen as contributing to this process was now broadened, obstacles other than entrenched business elites were recognized, and periods like the one preceding the New Deal were seen as having also had their reformist and constructive aspects.[17] The search from this quarter was for unrecognized reformers, unsuspected linkages between reform eras, and unexplored seedbeds of reform activity. And again, the search led to a new interest in and reexamination of the programs, policies, and activities with which Hoover had been associated.

As America moved into the 1960s, several other developments also helped to stimulate a rethinking of what was being written and taught about the nation's past. On the political right, neo-libertarian and neo-traditionalist movements appeared, both producing revised perceptions of established conservative heros.[18] From both came a rejection of the view that Hoover had championed the libertarian doctrines of laissez-faire and competitive individualism. And on the political left, the development of neo-Marxian perspectives created an intellectual context in which the ideas set forth by Broadus Mitchell and William Appleman Williams became the theoretical underpinning of new research. There's still another new framework emerged, stressing the constancies of class action, identifying imperialist designs masquerading as trade liberalization, and viewing pre-New Deal Republicanism as having, in many

[17] Of particular importance were Arthur S. Link, "What Happened to the Progressive Movement in the 1920's?" *American Historical Review* 64 (July 1959), 833-851; Clark A. Chambers, *Seed Time for Reform* (Minneapolis: University of Minnesota Press, 1963); Preston Hubbard, Jr., *Origins of the TVA* (Nashville: Vanderbilt University Press, 1961); Donald O. Swain, *Federal Conservation Policy, 1921-1933* (Berkeley: University of California Press, 1963); and George B. Tindall, "Business Progressivism," *South Atlantic Quarterly* 62 (Winter 1963), 92-106.

[18] See especially Murray Rothbard, *America's Great Depression* (Princeton: Van Nostrand, 1963); and Willmoore Kendall, *The Conservative Affirmation* (Chicago: Regnery, 1963).

ways, been wiser, more perceptive, and more sophisticated than the outlook that replaced it.[19] Men like Hoover, so a number of the new leftists held, were worth studying both as policy makers wrestling with the central contradictions of an advanced capitalist order and as prescient prophets of where liberal statism and efforts to export domestic difficulties could eventually lead.

By the mid-1960s, then, many historians were breaking away from the depression-born framework that had long inhibited serious study of the years during which Hoover had functioned as a national policy maker. If they could not agree upon what constituted the central story of modern America, they were no longer inclined to see the years from 1920 to 1932 as a barren and irrelevant interlude. What had once been treated as a backdrop or foil for the New Deal was now becoming important in its own right. It had become a new historiographical frontier for several streams of revisionist research and writing;[20] and together these were uncovering and seeking to understand a new and unfamiliar historical figure, a Herbert Hoover that bore much closer resemblances to the one perceived in 1929 or glimpsed by a few post-1933 revisionists than to the one depicted in New Deal polemics.

One obstacle that continued to hamper such research, however, was the thinness of the primary documentation to which historians had access. Collection and preservation policies, after all, had also been shaped by a framework emphasizing the importance of the Wilson and Roosevelt eras, not of what lay between them. And to most scholars, including most of those embracing revisionist perspectives, the materials collected and preserved in the Hoover papers remained closed. Not until 1966, following the establishment

---

[19] See Barton J. Bernstein, ed., *Towards a New Past* (New York: Random House, 1967).

[20] See Burl Noggle, "The Twenties: A New Historiographical Frontier," *Journal of American History* 53 (September 1966), 299-314.

of a new presidential library and the death of America's thirty-first president, did scholars finally gain access to materials documenting Hooverian policy making and illuminating its strategy for meeting modern needs through non-statist institutions.

III

Still, the years from 1959 through 1966 witnessed the appearance of several important works that not only reflected the weakening of conventional wisdom but also helped to shape the research and writing that followed. Six of these, in particular, stand out as efforts to apply revisionist insights to Hoover's public career. They became, to varying extents, part of a relevant literature in which those undertaking new research grounded themselves. And for these reasons, they deserve our attention and scrutiny.

The first of these new works to appear was Harris G. Warren's *Herbert Hoover and the Great Depression*.[21] Published in 1959, it depicted Hoover as a link between the old America and the new, primarily through his anti-depression measures. And while it retained much of the established framework, especially in its attribution of the depression to social reaction and accumulating business abuses, it also lingered over Hoover's reformist initiatives, his anticipation of New Deal measures, and his activism as a depression fighter. Hoover, so Warren concluded, had been the "greatest Republican of his generation." But even so, he had been incapable of seeing what was really needed, unable to control or contain the new forces that had entered the political arena, and too associated with big business to escape paying for its sins.

Two years after Warren's book appeared, William Appleman Williams offered a second and even more

---

[21] Harris G. Warren, *Herbert Hoover and the Great Depression* (New York: Oxford University Press, 1959).

influential reinterpretation of Hoover's public career. In a long section of his *Contours of American History*,[22] a section that built on ideas set forth in his earlier works, he depicted Hoover as the "keystone in the arch" leading from progressivism to the liberalism of the New and Fair Deals. He was, so Williams argued, the leading figure in a "corporate gentry" that had moved into the vanguard of progressive leadership and concerned itself with saving corporate capitalism from its own contradictions. In the face of the economic breakdown, he had "pulled out every antidepression tool the Progressives ever owned." Yet unlike Roosevelt, he could see the pitfalls inherent in statist supports and militant expansionism. From these he drew back, seeking a way that could avoid them, and he thus earned the opprobrium of those who could not see the dangers in what they were embracing. In Williams' scenario, Hoover remained an anti-Roosevelt. But he was not the anti-Roosevelt depicted in either New Deal celebrationism or the older defenses of his presidential policies.

In 1962, a year after the appearance of Williams' reinterpretation and three years after Warren's, a third work also took issue with the view that Hoover had become a laissez-faire ideologue clinging to an irrelevant past. His Commerce Department, so Joseph Brandes argued in his *Herbert Hoover and Economic Diplomacy*,[23] had been not only an efficient provider of business services but also a generator of associational and cooperative action, a reformer of the international marketplace, and an innovator in forging new diplomatic tools. A decade before the New Deal, it had developed government agencies geared to "the new requirements of large-scale American involvement in international economic affairs." And even though it had

[22]William Appleman Williams, *The Contours of American History* (Cleveland: World, 1961), 390-450.

[23]Joseph Brandes, *Herbert Hoover and Economic Diplomacy* (Pittsburgh: University of Pittsburgh Press, 1962).

failed to realize its vision of a world redeemed by American techniques and principles, it had assembled "an efficient corps of commercial attachés, trade commissioners, commodity chiefs, and bureau heads," all of whom "aided immeasurably in the achievement of American policies." For Brandes the Hoover years had been a creative and productive period in American economic diplomacy; and while some scholars remained unconvinced, clinging despite the evidence to images of "narrow economic nationalism" and "dismal" diplomacy,[24] others did find the argument persuasive and begin to wonder about other aspects of the conventional interpretation.

Still another work seeking to correct the conventional depiction of Hoover, although one that approached this task from a quite different angle, was Murray N. Rothbard's *America's Great Depression*.[25] Published in 1963, it found fault not with Hoover's conservative anti-statism but with his "audacious" departures from libertarian ideals and free-market economics. In Rothbard's account, Hoover was a corporate and statist planner, disguising himself as a voluntarist and free enterpriser, and taking actions that led directly to the evils of New Deal interventionism. He also bore much of the responsibility for the severity and persistence of the depression, not because he did too little, but because he did too much. Among the politicians and bureaucrats who had used the government to produce an unsound boom and obstruct healthy liquidation, he had clearly been the leader.

In the same year that Rothbard's book appeared, the historian Carl Degler also offered another seminal reinterpretation. Writing in the *Yale Review*,[26] he posed the same question that William Allen White had raised in 1933,

---

[24]See, for example, Alexander DeConde's review in *The American Historical Review* 68 (January 1963), 559.

[25]Cited in note 18.

[26]Carl Degler, "The Ordeal of Herbert Hoover," *Yale Review* 52 (Summer 1963), 563-583.

namely whether Hoover had been the "first of the new Presidents" or "the last of the old." This, so Degler suggested, could now be answered; and for him the answer could only be that Hoover had been both, that he was best understood as "a transition figure in the development of the government as an active force in the economy." His principles, both before and during his presidency, had been "distinctly and publicly progressive." He had always been careful to distinguish his views from the laissez-faire creed. And like Roosevelt, he had been a protegé of Woodrow Wilson, a borrower from the war model, a believer in business cycle control, and an optimist about the nation's capacity for economic growth and social justice. Yet at the same time, his progressivism had been narrowly circumscribed by ideological commitments to an older individualism and fiscal orthodoxy. If it had foreshadowed the actions of the New Deal, it had also insisted upon a thorough trial of privatist solutions and, in doing so, had convinced the public that something like the New Deal was the only alternative to continuing economic and social misery.

Similar arguments were also advanced two years later, when Albert U. Romasco published his *Poverty and Abundance: Hoover, the Nation and the Depression*.[27] Although still unable to use the Hoover papers, he offered the best documented account to date of the Hooverian recovery and relief programs, the financial and credit measures of 1931 and 1932, and the relationship that developed between the President, the Congress, and the press. All of these, as Romasco depicted them, had been shaped and limited by a rigid Hooverian ideology, which had blinded policy makers to economic and social realities, led them to opt for privatist solutions that had no chance of working, and rendered their strategies for maintaining political control increasingly

---

[27] Albert U. Romasco, *The Poverty of Abundance: Hoover, the Nation, and the Depression* (New York: Oxford University Press, 1965).

irrelevant. Yet the ideology involved had not been do-nothing-ism or a reliance on self-correction through the workings of natural economic laws. Hoover had believed that business cycles could be controlled and had acted on that belief. In this respect he was responsible for one of the most significant innovations in American history. He had also been a strong president, especially when it came to blocking those who were trying to substitute statist solutions for voluntaristic and community action. And in devising and organizing cooperative machinery that fitted the requirements of his creed, he had been an energetic and resourceful activist. The great irony of such actions was that they led not to more effective forms of economic and social self-government, as Hoover had intended, but to public convictions that recovery could come only through the use of federal power.

By the mid-1960s, then, a new body of writing on the Hoover years was clearly taking shape. It was not yet informed by the primary materials preserved in the Hoover papers. But it did reflect the new developments in American historiography, the growing tendency of what had once been a deviant revisionism to displace the established wisdom, and a new willingness to see Hoover as something other than an anti-Roosevelt wedded to laissez-faire dogma. One indication of the latter was the portrayal of Hoover in George Mowry's *The Urban Nation*,[28] a work published in 1965 as an interpretive synthesis of the four decades since 1920. In it Mowry accepted and built upon insights that had been associated with the historian Richard Hofstader. But Hoover was depicted less as a dogmatic defender of a dying philosophy than as an "enlightened conservative" and "twentieth-century industrial man" who had ruined himself politically on the issue of urban relief yet had gone "far along

---

[28]George E. Mowry, *The Urban Nation, 1920-1960* (New York: Hill & Wang, 1965).

the road" toward governmental intervention in the economic and social spheres.

IV

For students of Hoover's role in modern American history, the major event separating the last twenty-three years from their predecessors was the opening in 1966 of the collections preserved at the Hoover Presidential Library. Materials now became available for answering some of the questions raised by revisionist works and their perspective. And while books relatively unaffected by the new scholarship continued to appear, the focus of scholarly debate shifted increasingly to those who were examining the new materials in the light of revisionist perception.

Among the publications largely untouched by these scholarly debates were *The Shattered Dream* by Gene Smith and *Herbert Hoover: President of the United States* by Edgar Eugene Robinson and Vaughn Bornet.[29] Appearing respectively in 1970 and 1978, they retold the story of the Hoover presidency, adding new detail but diverging only in minor ways from the interpretive patterns set by partisan writers in the 1930s and 1940s. Smith, while depicting Hoover as a man of ideals and principles, found him calloused, insensitive, and essentially backward-looking, dreaming not of a new kind of modern society but of a social past rendered obsolete by twentieth-century developments. Writing primarily for a popular audience, Smith tended to draw much more heavily on depression mythology than on scholarly reevaluations. And Robinson and Bornet, while stressing Hoover's association with a new professional class and modern scientific values, insisted upon portraying the same paragon of virtue and wisdom as had appeared in the

---

[29]Gene Smith, *The Shattered Dream: Herbert Hoover and the Great Depression* (New York: Morrow, 1970); Edgar Eugene Robinson and Vaughn Bornet, *Herbert Hoover: President of the United States* (Stanford: Hoover Institution Press, 1975).

early works of Hoover partisans. The president that they depicted was not so much a transitional figure wrestling with modern dilemmas and paradoxes as he was a man of virtue and correct understanding, possessed of the wisdom that the nation needed but done in by character assassins, undisciplined congressional insurgents, and irresponsible political demagogues.

More affected by the new materials and insights were several studies focusing on Hoover's political performance and administrative style. In a reexamination of the election of 1928, David Burner rejected the established wisdom and emphasized the "provincialism" of Alfred E. Smith as contrasted with the cosmopolitianism of Herbert Hoover.[30] In a new study of congressional developments during the Hoover administration, Jordan Schwarz stressed the support for Hoover's positions and programs that had come from the Democratic legislative leadership.[31] In a book detailing Hoover's performance as a public relations manager, Craig Lloyd drew upon the newly opened materials at the Presidential Library to show how publicity systems became integral parts both of a personal administrative style and of an ideological prescription for national progress. Unfortunately, Lloyd concluded, the style and prescription served Hoover badly when he rose to the presidency and was confronted with depression conditions and the new political forces that they unleashed.[32] And in his works building on the insights of the political scientist Grant McConnell, Peri Arnold focused on Hoover's success in linking public agencies to

[30] David Burner, *The Politics of Provincialism: The Democratic Party in Transition, 1918-1932* (New York: Knopf, 1968), 179-216.

[31] Jordan A. Schwarz, *The Interregnum of Despair: Hoover, Congress, and the Depression* (Urbana: University of Illinois Press, 1970).

[32] Craig Lloyd, *Aggressive Introvert: Herbert Hoover and Public Relations Management* (Columbus: Ohio State University Press, 1972).

private government, thus creating a corporative administrative structure that has remained at the center of the American political system and has continued to frustrate democratic reform impulses.[33] In this sense, Arnold argued, modern America was less an extension of New Deal innovations than of those associated with Hoover's commerce secretariat and presidential initiatives.[34]

The view that Hoover was a bureaucratic innovator, seeking administrative structures that could meet modern needs without creating a burdensome state or destroying individual and local initiative, also received confirmation in a series of studies dealing with particular episodes and phases of his public career. Appearing between 1968 and 1973 were scholarly studies of his efforts to bring order to the coal industry, encourage social planning, regulate grain futures, provide disaster relief, mobilize credit resources, secure Indian reform measures, control oil pollution, and develop tools of macro-economic management,[35] all delineating

---

[33]Especially on the discussion of Hoover in Grant McConnell, *Private Power and American Democracy* (New York: Knopf, 1966).

[34]Peri Arnold, "Herbert Hoover and the Continuity of American Public Policy," *Public Policy* 20 (Fall 1972), 525-544. See also Peri Arnold, "Herbert Hoover and the Department of Commerce: A Study in Ideology and Policy," Ph.D. diss. (University of Chicago, 1972).

[35]Ellis W. Hawley, "Secretary Hoover and the Bituminous Coal Problem," *Business History Review* 42 (Autumn 1968), 253-270; Barry D. Karl, "Presidential Planning and Social Science Research," *Perspectives in American History* 3 (1969), 347-409; William R. Johnson, "Herbert Hoover and the Regulation of Grain Futures," *Mid-America* 51 (July 1969), 155-174; Bruce A. Lohoff, "Herbert Hoover: Spokesman of Humane Efficiency," *American Quarterly* 22 (Fall 1970), 690-700; James S. Olson, "The End of Voluntarism: Herbert Hoover and the National Credit Corporation," *Annals of Iowa* 41 (Fall 1972), 1104-1113; Kenneth Philip, "Herbert Hoover's New Era: a False Dawn for the American Indian," *Rocky Mountain Social Science Journal* 9 (April 1972), 53-60; Douglas Drake, "Herbert Hoover, Ecologist: The Politics of Oil Pollution Control, 1921-1926," *Mid-America* 55 (July 1973), 207-228; Carolyn Grin, "The

organizational designs that in theory could provide the benefits of modern management without incurring the evils associated with monopoly, regimentation, or bureaucratic centralism. During the same period such books as Robert Zieger's *The Republicans and Labor*, Herbert Stein's *The Fiscal Revolution in America*, and Edwin Layton's *The Revolt of the Engineers*[36] offered further evidence of Hoover's affiliation, despite his anti-statism, with technocratic and planning impulses. And in 1974, in an article delineating and analyzing his transformation of the Commerce secretariat,[37] he was depicted as the would-be builder of a modernizing associationalism, seeking to meet modern needs through associative as opposed to statist actions and seeking in particular to build social units that combined technocratic planning and corporative discipline with the voluntary action of free individuals. What scholars were now accepting as reality was not completely in line with the perceptions of those writing contemporary history in March of 1929. But clearly, it bore a much closer resemblance to such perceptions than to those associated with Hoover's subsequent disparagers and defenders.

What was true of domestic policy studies also had its counterpart in foreign policy studies. Here the view of Republican diplomacy previously advanced by William Appleman Williams was not fully substantiated. But such scholars as Carl Parrini, Joan Hoff Wilson, Melvyn Leffler, and Michael J. Hogan were documenting the existence of

Unemployment Conference of 1921: An Experiment in National Cooperative Planning," *Mid-America* 55 (April 1973), 83-107.

[36]Robert H. Zieger, *Republicans and Labor, 1919-1929* (Lexington; University Press of Kentucky, 1969); Herbert Stein, *The Fiscal Revolution in America* (Chicago: University of Chicago Press, 1969); Edwin T. Layton, Jr., *The Revolt of the Engineers* (Cleveland: Case Western Reserve University Press, 1971).

[37]Ellis W. Hawley, "Herbert Hoover, the Commerce Secretariat, and the Vision of an 'Associative State,' 1921-1928," *Journal of American History* 61 (June 1974), 116-140.

techno-corporative ideals, delineating their roles in shaping and sustaining policy decisions, and showing how the notion of a Republican withdrawal into isolationism and inaction had indeed been a "legend."[38] As in the domestic sphere, they noted, the search had been for stimulative and coordinating mechanisms that in theory could bring forward nonstatist agencies capable of realizing Wilsonian goals. And like Williams, they portrayed the men engaged in this exercise not as blind fools, naive utopians, or hoodwinkers of the public but as sophisticated and perceptive students of the international order. Hoover, in particular, was credited with having seen both the connections between capitalist behavior and political disorder and the evils that could flow from using statist power to deal with the resulting problems.

While such studies were appearing, two collaborative works also provided indications of the kind of scholarly activity and debate that was now taking place. Published in 1973 in the American Forum series, *Herbert Hoover and the Crisis of American Capitalism*[39] contained essays in which Murray Rothbard, Gerald Nash, Robert Himmelberg, and Ellis Hawley offered reinterpretations of Hoover's political philosophy and public career. And while these reflected important disagreements, particularly in regard to the sincerity of Hoover's anti-statism, his performance as a politician, and his commitment to competitive ideals, all rejected depictions

---

[38] Carl P. Parrini, *Heir to Empire: United States Economic Diplomacy, 1916-1923* (Pittsburgh: University of Pittsburgh Press, 1969); Joan Hoff Wilson, *American Business and Foreign Policy, 1920-1933* (Lexington: University of Kentucky Press, 1971); Melvyn P. Leffler, "Political Isolationism, Economic Expansion, or Diplomatic Realism," *Perspectives in American History* 8 (1974), 413-461; Michael J. Hogan, "Informal Entente: Public Policy and Private Management in Anglo-American Petroleum Affairs," *Business History Review* 48 (Summer 1974), 187-205.

[39] J. Joseph Huthmacher and Warren I. Sussman, eds., *Herbert Hoover and the Crisis of American Capitalism: Essays and Rejoinders by Ellis W. Hawley, Murray N. Rothbard, Robert F. Himmelberg, and Gerald D. Nash* (Cambridge: Schenkman, 1973).

of Hoover as a champion and defender of laissez-faire. He appeared instead as the "progressive" champion of an associative, corporatist, or mixed economy, seeking tools for the management of "progress" and accepting much of the ideological structure associated with progressive thought. Such was the case as well in most of the essays contained in *The Hoover Presidency: A Reappraisal*,[40] a collection published in 1974 following the participation of interested scholars in a conference at Geneseo, New York. Here, as in the Forum essays, Hoover's activist, managerial, and reformist inclinations were much in evidence with the disagreement coming more over their suitability and effects than over their existence. Only in the essay by Selig Adler was there a disposition to discount much of the revisionist scholarship and see it as being motivated by a desire to discredit Franklin D. Roosevelt and his works.

Still another indication of the kinds of revisionism now under way came at a series of scholarly seminars held in 1974 in conjunction with the centennial of Hoover's birth. Meeting at the Hoover Presidential Library, these focused in turn on the war period, seeking in each instance to pull together and assess what researchers were finding. And while some of the papers tended toward celebrationism or towards defenses of the claims made in the "conservative" history of the 1930s and 1940s, most of them reflected the various streams of revisionism that had emerged in the 1960s.[41] Again Hoover

---

[40]Martin L. Fausold and George T. Mazuzan, eds., *The Hoover Presidency: a Reappraisal* (Albany: State University of New York Press, 1974). The essays were by Donald R. McCoy, David Burner, Albert Romasco, Jordan Schwarz, Ellis Hawley, Alfred B. Rollins, Frank Freidel, Selig Adler, and Joan Hoff Wilson.

[41]The papers, currently held by the Hoover Presidential Library Association, were given by Robert D. Cuff, Witold Sworakowski, Royal J. Schmidt, Murray N. Rothbard, Eugene Trani, Robert Van Meter, Carl Parrini, Robert F. Himmelberg, Francis W. O'Brien, Robert K. Murray, Ellis Hawley, Joan Hoff Wilson, Robert Zieger, George W. Carey, Joseph Brandes, Melvyn Leffler, Barry Karl, Arthur Kemp, Alexander DeConde, John Schmidhauser, Justin Green, Martin Fausold, Frank Friedel, Carl Christol, David Burner, Richard

appeared not as a laissez-faire ideologue of business fundamentalism but as a man engrossed in the problems of ordering and managing the forces of modernization, seeking solutions in associative, corporative, and partnership mechanisms, and working assiduously to develop a planning and welfare apparatus that would remain free of the evils inherent in statist or socialist prescriptions. If judgements still diferred about the perceptiveness, consequences and current relevance of the Hooverian approach there appeared to be wide agreement about its general nature, about its combination of managerial optimism with assumptions of statist incompetence, and about its being a part of some larger reformist, managerial, stabilizing, or corporative impulse.

Similar generalizations could also be made about the subsequent publications of seminar participants and other scholars. Appearing in print now were new studies of the Reconstruction Finance Corporation, the Smoot-Hawley Tariff, and the Bonus Army episode,[42] of Hoover as war manager, agricultural policy maker, relief mobilizer, and originator of macroeconomic management,[43] of his approach

N. Kottman, Malcolm Moos, Donald R. McCoy, Russell Ross, Charles Cary, William A. Williams, and Morton Frisch. Eight papers have been published in Lawrence Gelfand, ed., *Herbert Hoover: The Great War and Its Aftermath, 1914-1923* (Iowa City: University of Iowa Press, 1979). Seven more appear in Ellis Hawley, ed., *Herbert Hoover as Secretary of Commerce, 1921-1928* (Iowa City: University of Iowa Press, 1981).

[42]James S. Olson, *Herbert Hoover and the Reconstruction Finance Corporation, 1931-1933* (Ames: Iowa State University Press, 1977); Richard N. Kottman, "Herbert Hoover and the Smoot-Hawley Tariff: Canada, A Case Study," *Journal of American History* 62 (December 1975), 609-635; Donald J. Lisio, *The President and Protest: Hoover, Conspiracy, and the Bonus Riot* (Columbia: University of Missouri Press, 1974).

[43]Robert D. Cuff, "Herbert Hoover, the Ideology of Voluntarism, and War Organization During the Great War," *Journal of American History* 64 (September 1977), 358-372; Robert D. Cuff, "The Dilemmas of Voluntarism: Hoover and the Pork-Packing Agreement of 1917-1919," *Agricultural History* 53 (October 1979), 727-747; Joan Hoff Wilson, "Hoover's Agricultural Policies, 1921-1928," *Agricultural History* 51 (April 1977), 335-361; Martin J. Fausold,

to labor and racial questions,[44] of his activities and images during the last years of the Wilson administration,[45] and of the moral principles he had come to espouse.[46] In addition, he appeared as a central figure in new studies of the trade association issue, Republican era diplomacy, welfare capitalism, and corporate liberalism.[47] And helping to

"President Hoover's Farm Policies, 1929-1933," *Agricultural History* 51 (April 1977), 362-377; Gary H. Koerselman, "Secretary Hoover and National Farm Policy," *Agricultural History* 51 (April 1977), 378-395; C. Roger Lambert, "Hoover, the Red Cross, and Food for the Hungry," *Annals of Iowa* 64 (Winter 1979), 530-540; Evan B. Metcalf, "Secretary Hoover and the Emergence of Macroeconomic Management," *Business History Review* 49 (Spring 1975), 60-80.

[44]Robert H. Zieger, "Labor, Progressivism, and Herbert Hoover," *Wisconsin Magazine of History* 58 (Spring 1975), 196-208; Zieger, "Herbert Hoover, the Wage-Earner, and the 'New Economic System,' 1919-1929," *Business History Review* 51 (Summer 1977), 161-189; George F. Garcia, "Herbert Hoover and the Issue of Race," *Annals of Iowa* 64 (Winter 1979), 507-517.

[45]Gary Dean Best, *The Politics of American Individualism: Herbert Hoover in Transition, 1918-1921* (Westport: Greenwood, 1975); Robert F. Himmelberg, "Hoover's Public Image, 1919-1920," in Gelfand, ed., *Hoover, 1914-23*, pp. 209-232.

[46]David Burner and Thomas R. West, "A Technocrat's Morality: Conservatism and Hoover the Engineer," in Stanley Elkins and Eric McKitrick, eds., *The Hofstadter Aegis* (New York: Knopf, 1974), 235-256.

[47]Robert F. Himmelberg, *The Origins of the National Recovery Administration: Business, Government and the Trade Association Issue, 1921-1933* (New York: Fordham University Press, 1976); Michael J. Hogan, *Informal Entente: The Private Structure of Cooperation in Anglo-American Economic Diplomacy, 1918-1928* (Columbia: University of Missouri Press, 1977); Melvyn P. Leffler, *The Elusive Quest: America's Pursuit of European Stability and French Security, 1919-1933* (Chapel Hill: University of North Carolina Press, 1979); Benjamin Rhodes, "Herbert Hoover and the War Debts, 1919-1933," *Prologue* 6 (Summer 1974), 150-180; Kim McQuaid, "Corporate Liberalism in the American Business Community, 1920-1940," *Business History Review* 52 (Autumn 1978), 342-368; Ellis W. Hawley, "Le nouveau coporatisme et les democrates liberales, 1878-1925; les cas des Etats-Unis," *Revue Recherches* (September 1978), 325-344.

confirm the ongoing reinterpretation were new documentary publications, notably of the public papers of his presidency and of his correspondence with Woodrow Wilson.[48] In volume the continuing stream of scholarship was impressive, reflecting, it seemed, both a heightened interest in the Hoover era and a heightened appreciation of its historical significance and current relevance. And in findings, the triumph of revisionist views over the older "liberal" and "conservative" perspectives seemed increasingly apparent. While scholarly interpreters still arrived at differing assessments of Hoover's public actions and of the relationship between his programs and those of the New Deal, they seemed increasingly convinced of his modernism, activism, reformism, and managerialism.

Such perceptions were also evident in two new biographies of Hoover. Published in 1975, Joan Hoff Wilson's *Herbert Hoover: Forgotten Progressive*[49] provided a much needed synthesis of recent scholarship, broke new ground in relating the altered perceptions of his public career to his earlier and later life, and concluded that there was much to be said for the "new day" he was seeking to develop in the 1920s. He had, she thought, understood the problems and alternative organizational futures of America far better than most of his contemporaries. And in *Herbert Hoover: A Public Life*,[50] published in 1979, David Burner again emphasized how Hoover's business and public careers had

---

[48]*Public Papers of the Presidents of the United States: Herbert Hoover, 1929-1933*, 4 vols. (Washington: GPO, 1974-1977); Francis W. O'Brien, ed., *The Hoover-Wilson Wartime Correspondence* (Ames: Iowa State University Press, 1974); Francis W. O'Brien, ed., *Two Peacemakers in Paris: The Hoover-Wilson Post-Armistice Letters* (College Station: Texas A&M University Press, 1978).

[49]Joan Hoff Wilson, *Herbert Hoover: Forgotten Progressive* (Boston: Little Brown, 1975).

[50]David Burner, *Herbert Hoover: A Public Life* (New York: Knopf, 1979).

been intertwined with the rise and functioning of modern organizational institutions. While pointing up a series of flaws in Hoover's ideas and programs, Burner interpreted them as a developing progressivism, seeking to impose enlightened order on ever-larger spheres of activity and manifesting itself in a broad array of administrative innovations, reform initiatives, and promotional endeavors. Like other forms of progressivism, it was to be understood as an effort to make modern forms of collectivity serve the ends envisioned in nineteenth-century liberalism.

Whether in biographies, specialized monographs, or period surveys,[51] the Hoover of depression rhetoric and "liberal" history was now losing scholarly creditability. Yet to the dismay of some who had long complained about misrepresentation, the gains in creditability were less for the hero of "conservative" history than for the figure perceived by the interpreters of 1929 and the deviant revisionists of the next three decades. The new scholarship offered little support for claims that Hoover's depression remedies had been effective. Nor was it validating claims of almost infallible wisdom and virtually unblemished virtue. But once again it was becoming difficult to argue that Hoover had not been in the mainstream of modern American development, that he had remained outside the technocratic and planning impulses emanating from a modern administrative elite, or that his conceptions of alternative organizational futures had been hopelessly flawed by outmoded ideological commitments.

---

[51]See, for example, David A. Shannon, *Between the Wars: America, 1919-1941* (Boston: Houghton Mifflin, 1979 ed.); William H. Wilson, *Coming of Age, Urban America, 1915-1945* (New York: Wiley, 1974); Donald R. McCoy, *Coming of Age: The United States during the 1920's and 1930's* (Baltimore: Penguin, 1973); and Ellis W. Hawley, *The Great War and the Search for a Modern Order: A History of the American People and Their Institutions, 1917-1933* (New York: St. Martin's Press, 1979).

V

In the years since 1979, the study and interpretation of Herbert Hoover have, for the most part, followed patterns established in the 1970s. The images associated with progressive and conservative have persisted to some extent in scholarly criticism of revisionist work[52] and with great tenacity in the national political culture and the discourse that it has informed. But most of the new scholarship has been "revisionist" in the sense that it has rejected these images and recognized Hoover's activism, modernism, and efforts to create new institutional machinery. Although interpretive quarrels have persisted, they have been mostly over evaluations and explanations of this activism, modernism, and attempted institution building, not over their existence.

Such has been the case with continuing biographical work and continuing study of presidential performance. The former has been concerned chiefly with reconstructing and reinterpreting Hoover's engineering, business, and post-presidential careers and has found in them an individual closer to the revisionist picture than to those in progressive or conservative history.[53] And the latter, as expressed in the work of the historian Martin Fausold and the economist William Barber, has had a similarly revisionist cast, one that has found a place for such revisionist conceptions as the "corporatist balance," the "reform presidency," the "associative state," and a proto-Keynesian "new

---

[52]See, for example, Elliot Rosen's review of Ellis W. Hawley, ed., *Herbert Hoover as Secretary of Commerce*, in *The Historian* 66 (November 1983), 131-132.

[53]The most prominent biographical works have been George H. Nash, *The Life of Herbert Hoover: The Engineer, 1874-1914* (New York: Norton, 1983); Gary Dean Best, *Herbert Hoover: The Post-Presidential Years* (Stanford: Hoover Institution Press, 1983); and Richard Norton Smith, *An Uncommon Man: The Triumph of Herbert Hoover* (New York: Simon & Schuster, 1984).

economics."[54] Yet within the new scholarship, several questions have remained controversial and unsettled. The revisionists, for example, have not agreed about the importance of Quakerism in shaping Hoover's world view and policy prescriptions;[55] they have differed over the extent to which the approach associated with psycho-biography can help us to understand his public career;[56] and they have diverged widely in their judgements about the mixture of wisdom and fallacy to be found in the revised record of his thought and activities.[57]

[54] See Martin L. Fausold, *The Presidency of Herbert C. Hoover* (Lawrence: University Press of Kansas, 1985) and William J. Barber, *From New Era to New Deal: Herbert Hoover, the Economists, and American Economic Policy, 1921-1933* (New York: Cambridge University Press, 1985). See also Ellis W. Hawley, "Herbert Hoover, 1929-1933," in Frank N. Magill and John L. Loos, eds., *The American Presidents: The Office and the Men* (Pasadena: Salem Press, 1986), 555-574.

[55] Compare, for example, the downplaying of Quakerism in Nash's *Hoover: The Engineer* with the emphasis on it in Fausold's *Presidency of Hoover*. See also the contrasting views in the essays by David Burner and Ellis Hawley in Lee Nash, ed., *Understanding Herbert Hoover* (Stanford: Hoover Institution Press, 1987).

[56] Recent efforts to apply elements of the psycho-biography approach have included James P. Johnson, "Herbert Hoover and David Copperfield: A Tale of Two Childhoods," *Journal of Psychohistory* 7 (Spring 1980), 467-475; Kendrick A. Clements, "Herbert Hoover and the Fish," *Journal of Psychohistory* 10 (Winter 1983), 333-348; and James P. Johnson, "Herbert Hoover: The Orphan as Children's Friend," *Prologue* 12 (Winter 1980), 193-206. Another work helping to illuminate personality traits as they were translated into political strategies is Rosanne Sizer, "Herbert Hoover and the Smear Books," *Annals of Iowa* 47 (Spring 1984), 343-361.

[57] As in the 1970s, the new scholarship has tended to view the increasingly well documented activism and modernism as virtuous but has had both positive and negative things to say about prescriptions for containing the growth of "statism." It has also left largely intact and in some respects even strengthened what earlier critics had to say about Hoover's ideological rigidity, insecure defensiveness, penchant for manipulation, and ineptitude for partisan and mass politics.

What is true of biographical work and accounts of the presidency has also been true of a continuing flow of scholarship prepared for conference presentations and published in collections of scholarly essays. Since 1979 four such collections have appeared, one making available more of the essays prepared for the Hoover Centennial Seminars,[58] a second assembled through the initiative of Senator Mark Hatfield,[59] a third featuring work done in Martin Fausold's NEH Seminar at the Hoover Presidential Library,[60] and a fourth consisting of essays commissioned for a series of Hoover Symposia at George Fox College.[61] As in the case

---

[58]Ellis W. Hawley, ed., *Herbert Hoover as Secretary of Commerce, 1921-1928: Studies in New Era Thought and Practice* (Iowa City: University of Iowa Press, 1981). The collection contained essays on Hoover's role in the Cabinet (Robert K. Murray), on his activities in shaping business, labor, agricultural, and diplomatic policy (Hawley, Robert H. Zieger, Joan Hoff Wilson, Melvyn P. Leffler, and Joseph Brandes), and on his thinking concerning individualism (George W. Carey). All but the last were in the revisionist mold; and its "conservatism," which took the form of applying the analytical conceptions of Leo Strauss to Hoover's thought, was not of the usual variety.

[59]*Herbert Hoover Reassessed: Essays Commemorating the Fiftieth Anniversary of the Inauguration of Our Thirty-first President* (Washington: GPO, 1981). A number of essays had been previously published. But among the leading ones that had not been were Frank Freidel, "Hoover and Roosevelt and Historical Continuity;" Gary Dean Best, "Herbert Hoover, 1933-1941: A Reassessment;" Alexander DeConde, "Herbert Hoover, 1933-1941: A Reassessment;" and Donald R. McCoy, "Herbert Hoover and Foreign Policy, 1939-1945."

[60]Carl E. Krog and William R. Tanner, eds., *Herbert Hoover and the Republican Era: A Reconsideration* (Lanham, Md.: University Press of America, 1984). Included were essays on Hoover's anti-waste campaign (Tanner), aviation program (David D. Lee), recreational policies (Krog), Indian reforms (William G. Robbins), racial attitudes (Larry Grothaus), agricultural programs (C. Roger Lambert and Bernard M. Klass), and relations with Gerald P. Nye (David A. Horowitz).

[61]Lee Nash, ed., *Understanding Herbert Hoover: Ten Perspectives* (Stanford: Hoover Institution Press, 1987). The ten perspectives are

of most such collections, these suffer from unevenness, discontinuity, and somewhat strained efforts to achieve a degree of unity. But they contain some excellent scholarship, and they are clearly reflective of the tendency to embrace revisionist conceptions while disagreeing as to how the revised record should be explained and evaluated. In general, the essays have discovered and documented further manifestations of Hoover's activism, managerial ethos, and associational thinking and endeavor. Yet the essayists have been of different minds in their analysis and assessments of these discoveries. For some the emphasis has been on their progressive, reformist, and foreward-looking tendencies; but for others it has been on their inadequacies, blind spots, and incompatibility with the need for new kinds of governmental intervention and activity.

The same general pattern has also been apparent in scholarship that has taken the form of monographs, journal articles, and parts of books on such subjects as regulation, progressivism, peace-keeping, presidential management, business cycle control, and economic diplomacy. It was the revisionist depiction of Hoover that appeared in new studies of his administrative theory and practice,[62] of his handling of sick or problem industries,[63] of his welfare, conservation,

---

those of Joan Hoff Wilson, George H. Nash, Mark O. Hatfield, David Burner, Ellis W. Hawley, Susan Estebrook Kennedy, Gary Dean Best, Frank Freidel, Robert E. Burke, and William G. Robbins.

[62]Peri Arnold, "The 'Great Engineer' as Administrator: Herbert Hoover and Modern Bureaucracy," *Review of Politics* 42 (July 1980), 328-348; Ronald C. Moe, *The Hoover Commissions Revisited* (Boulder: Westview, 1982); Tom G. Hall, "Government Controls: How to Understand the Experience of World War I," in Trudy H. Peterson, ed, *Farmers, Bureaucrats and Middlemen* (Washington: Howard University Press, 1980). See also, William E. Pemberton, *Bureaucratic Politics: Executive Reorganization during the Truman Administration* (Columbia: University of Missouri Press, 1979); and Peri E. Arnold, *Making the Managerial Presidency: Comprehensive Reorganization Planning, 1905-1980* (Princeton: Princeton University Press, 1986).

[63]Ellis Hawley, "Three Facets of Hooverian Associationalism: Lumber, Aviation, and Movies, 1921-1930," in Thomas K. McCraw,

and drought relief policies,[64] and of his post-presidential progressivism, prescriptions for lasting peace, and record as

---

ed., *Regulation in Perspective: Historical Essays* (Boston: Harvard Business School, 1981); David D. Lee, "Herbert Hoover and the Development of Commercial Aviation, 1921-1926," *Business History Review* 58 (Spring 1984), 78-102; William G. Robbins, "Voluntary Cooperation v. Regulatory Paternalism: The Lumber Trade in the 1920s," *Business History Review* 56 (Autumn 1982), 358-379; Robbins, *Lumberjacks and Legislators: Political Economy of the U.S. Lumber Industry, 1890-1941* (College Station: Texas A&M University Press, 1982), esp. pp. 112-132; James L. Guth, "Herbert Hoover, the U.S. Food Administration and the Dairy Industry," *Business History Review* 55 (Summer 1981), 170-187; Philip T. Rosen, *The Modern Stentors: Radio Broadcasters and the Federal Government, 1920-1934,* (Westport: Greenwood Press, 1980); David E. Hamilton, "From New Era to New Deal: American Farm Policy Between the Wars," in Lawrence Gelfand and Robert Neymeyer, eds., *Agricultural Distress and the Midwest: Past and Present* (Iowa City: Center for the Study of the Recent History of the United States, 1986).

[64]James N. Giglio, "Voluntarism and Public Policy Between World War I and the New Deal: Herbert Hoover and the American Child Health Association," *Presidential Studies Quarterly* 13 (Summer 1983), 430-452; Vaughn Davis Bornet, "Herbert Hoover's Planning for Unemployment and Old Age Insurance Coverage, 1921 to 1933," in John N. Schacht, ed., *The Quest for Security: Papers on the Origins and the Future of the American Social Insurance System* (Iowa City: Center for the Study of the Recent History of the United States, 1982), 35-71; William H. Mullins, "Self Help in Seattle, 1931-32: Herbert Hoover's Concept of Cooperative Individualism and the Unemployed Citizen's League," *Pacific Northwest Quarterly* 72 (January 1981), 11-19; William G. Robbins, "Herbert Hoover's Indian Reformers under Attack: The Failures of Administrative Reform," *Mid-America* 63 (October 1981), 157-170; Carl Krog, "'Organizing the Production of Leisure:' Herbert Hoover and the Conservation movements of the 1920s," *Wisconsin Magazine of History* 67 (Spring 1984), 199-218; Kendrick Clements, "Herbert Hoover and Conservation, 1921-1933," *American Historical Review* 89 (February 1984), 67-88; David E. Hamilton, "Herbert Hoover and the Great Drought of 1930," *Journal of American History* 68 (March 1982), 850-875; Nan Elizabeth Woodruff, *As Rare as Rain: Federal Relief in the Great Southern Drought of 1930-1931* (Champaign: University of Illinois Press, 1985).

a writer.⁶⁵ It was a Hoover trying to implement designs for racial and regional progress, not one intent upon keeping blacks in their place, that Donald Lisio reconstructed and documented in his exhaustively researched and carefully argued study of the presidency's Southern strategies.⁶⁶ And it was the revisionist Hoover, seeking to coax from the private sector a substitute for the modern state, that appeared in new studies of the period's search for macroeconomic

---

⁶⁵Joan Hoff Wilson,, "Herbert Hoover's Progressive Response to the New Deal," in John N. Schacht, ed., *Three Progressives from Iowa: Gilbert N. Haugen, Herbert C. Hoover, and Henry A. Wallace* (Iowa City: Center for the Study of the Recent History of the United States, 1980), 17-35; George H. Nash, "The Mind of a Peacemaker;" Gary Dean Best, "Herbert Hoover and Postwar Foreign Policy;" and Joan Hoff Wilson, "The Postwar World According to Hoover," all in Thomas T. Thalken, ed., *The Problems of a Lasting Peace Revisited* (West Branch: Herbert Hoover Presidential Library Association, 1986); Wilton Eckley, *Herbert Hoover* (Boston: Twayne, 1980).

⁶⁶Donald J. Lisio, *Hoover, Blacks, & Lily-Whites: A Study in Southern Strategies* (Chapel Hill: University of North Carolina Press, 1985). See also David S. Day, "Herbert Hoover and Racial Politics: The DePriest Incident," *Journal of Negro History* 65 (Winter 1980), 6-17; George F. Garcia, "Black Disaffection from the Republican Party during the Presidency of Herbert Hoover, 1928-1932," *Annals of Iowa* 45 (Fall 1980), 462-497; David J. Ginzl, "Patronage, Race, and Politics: Georgia Republicans During the Hoover Administration," *Georgia Historical Quarterly* 64 (Fall 1980), 280-293; Ginzl, "Lily-Whites versus Black-and-Tans: Mississippi Republicans during the Hoover Administration," *Journal of Mississippi History* 62 (Fall 1980), 194-211; Ginzl, "The Politics of Patronage: Florida Republicans during the Hoover Administration," *Florida Historical Quarterly* 61 (Spring 1982), 1-19.

⁶⁷Guy Alchon, *The Invisible Hand of Planning: Capitalism, Social Science, and the State in the 1920s* (Princeton: Princeton University Press, 1985); Udo Sautter, "Government and Unemployment: The Use of Public Works before the New Deal," *Journal of American History* 73 (June 1986), 59-86; Frank Costigliola, *Awkward Dominion: American Economic, Political, and Cultural Relations with Europe, 1919-1933* (Ithaca: Cornell University Press, 1984); Emily S. Rosenberg, *Spreading the American Dream: American Economic and Cultural Expansion, 1890-1945* (New York: Hill & Wang, 1982); Edward D. Berkowitz and Kim McQuaid, "Bureaucrats

stabilization, international order, non-statist welfare agencies, and tools for coping with market failures in particular industries.[67] With few exceptions, the producers of this scholarship found the revisionist picture of Hoover more credible than its long-standing rivals.[68] Yet again, agreement on this was not accompanied by agreement on whether the Hooverian designs and deeds now accepted as historical reality deserved praise for their prescience and sophistication, condemnation for their naivete and inadequacy, or contemplation for what they revealed about underlying social forces and tensions. One could find some of each.[69]

There was evidence, moreover, that scholars working on other periods or engaged in writing larger surveys were aware of and were beginning to accept the revisionist depiction of Hoover. His standing, to be sure, did not rise in polls asking historians of the United States to rank presidents in terms of how well they had filled the office. They could still find twenty presidents that they would rank above him.[70]

---

as Social Engineers: Federal Welfare Programs in Herbert Hoover's America," *American Journal of Economics and Sociology* 39 (October 1980), 321-335; Ellis W. Hawley, "'Industrial Policy' in the 1920s and 1930s," in Claude Barfield and William Schambra, eds., *The Politics of Industrial Policy* (Washington: American Enterprise Institute, 1986), 63-86; Robert F. Himmelberg, "Government and Business, 1917-1932," in Joseph Frese and Jacob Judd, eds., *Business and Government: Essays in 20th Century Cooperation and Confrontation* (Tarrytown: Sleepy Hollow Press, 1985), 1-23; Peri E. Arnold, "Herbert Hoover and the Positive State," in David Greenstone, ed., *Public Values and Private Power in American Politics* (Chicago: University of Chicago Press, 1982), 109-138.

[68]One notable exception, advancing a counter-revisionist argument concerning Hoover's Latin American policies, is E.R. Curry, *Hoover's Dominican Diplomacy and the Origins of the Good Neighbor Policy* (New York: Garland, 1979).

[69]Mixtures of the three could be found in most of the works cited. But the makeup of the mixtures varied considerably. Nash, Best, Hoff Wilson, Rosen, and Bornet, although they wrote from different perspectives, tended to be the most sympathetic, while Robbins, Clements, Woodruff, Garcia, and Hamilton were among those tending to put the stress on inadequacies.

[70]Robert K. Murray and Tim H. Blessing, "The Presidential Performance Study: A Progress Report," *Journal of American History*

But this did not measure the advance of revisionism, one form of which rejected the images of "do-nothingism" and "stand-pattery" while still seeing Hoover as lacking what the nation needed in its presidential office in the early 1930s.[71] A better measure is the discussions of Hooverian activism and organizational endeavor that have begun to appear in surveys of United States history and twentieth century America, in treatments of the contemporary world, and in some recent accounts of the New Deal, Truman era diplomacy, and President Dwight D. Eisenhower's search for a "middle way."[72] These seem to represent a growing

---

70 (December 1983), 535-555. In the Schlesinger polls of 1948 and 1962, Hoover had ranked respectively twentieth and nineteenth. Nor did Murray and Blessing think that Hoover's standing was likely to rise in the future, primarily because they found that younger historians rated him lower than older ones. They did note, however, a wide divergence of judgement among the polled, one that made him the third-most controversial of the presidents and might possibly indicate that a change was underway.

[71] See, for example, David D. Lee, "The Politics of Less: The Trials of Herbert Hoover and Jimmy Carter," *Presidential Studies Quarterly* 13 (Spring 1983), 305-312, which finds striking similarities between the "new Hoover" of revisionist scholarship and another presidential "failure"—i.e. James Earl Carter.

[72] See, for example, Robert Divine and others, *America: Past and Present* (Glenview: Scott, Foreman, 1986); David W. Noble, and others, *Twentieth Century Limited: A History of Recent America* (Boston: Houghton Mifflin, 1980), David R. Contosta and Robert Muccigrosso, *America in the Twentieth Century: Coming of Age* (New York: Harper & Row, 1988), Paul Johnson, *Modern Times: The World from the Twenties to the Eighties* (New York: Harper & Row, 1983); Robert S. McElvaine, *The Great Depression: America, 1929-1941* (New York: Times Books, 1984), chapter 3; Alan Brinkley, "The New Deal: Prelude," *Wilson Quarterly* 6 (Spring 1982), 50-61; Michael J. Hogan, *The Marshall Plan: America, Britain, and the Reconstruction of Western Europe, 1947-1952* (New York: Cambridge University Press, 1987); Robert Griffith, "Dwight D. Eisenhower and the Corporate Commonwealth," *American Historical Review* 87 (February 1982), 87-122.

scholarly conviction that the "new Hoover" portrayed in the continuing flow of revisionist scholarship is the real one.[73]

Still, as the historian Robert Himmelberg has noted, the "new Hoover" has remained "almost exclusively a scholar's Hoover." Outside of scholarly circles, particularly in letters to the editor and most journalistic writing, in "the folk history of the American people," and in political speeches and other discourse informed by the political culture, the "old, laissez-faire Hoover" (the villain of progressive history and the hero of its conservative rival) has remained very much alive.[74] It is the "old Hoover" that gets invoked when the stock market plunges, when the Democrats attack Republican conservatism and call for another New Deal, or when debate over the workings of the welfare and regulatory state becomes heated and begins using "history" to support its arguments.[75] And ironically, in so far as the "new Hoover" has been able to penetrate the political culture at all, this has tended to undercut conservative mythology more than it has the liberal variety. The "supply siders" who came to power with the Reagan administration did accept the basic outlines of the "new Hoover" but having done so proceeded to read him out of the conservative pantheon, substitute the likes of Andrew Mellon and Calvin Coolidge, and conclude that he had, after all, caused the Great Depression.[76]

[73] For a good commentary on "the Hoover industry" and its portrayal of a "new Hoover," see Himmelberg, "Government and Business, 1917-32," In Joseph Frese and Jacob Judd, eds. *Business and Government*, 2-6.

[74] Ibid., 3. See also Joan Hoff Wilson, "Herbert Hoover: The Popular Image of an Unpopular President," in Nash, ed., *Understanding Herbert Hoover*, 3-23.

[75] This was especially true of the rhetoric that accompanied the elections of 1980, 1982, and 1984 and of that accompanying the stock market plunge of October 1987. But one could note exceptions—politicians, for example, like Mark Hatfield or journalists like Hugh Sidey. See Tom Walsh, "Herbert Hoover Reassessed," *Ripon Forum* (June 1987), and Hugh Sidey, "The Hands-On Manager," *Time* (November 9, 1987).

[76] See Jude Wanniski, *The Way the World Works: How Economics Fail—And Succeed* (New York: Basic Books, 1978); George Nash,

The persistence of negative imagery, moreover, made it unlikely that the "new Hoover" would enter the pantheon of those who were again searching for a "middle way," a way, in particular, that could use a combination of technical expertise and public-private partnerships to render the nation's "industrial policy" more coherent, "revitalize" its developmental impulses, "reindustrialize" its economic base, and enhance its "competitiveness" in export markets. Scholars could point out the similarities of the designs being offered to those that Hoover had sought to implement; and a few of those engaged in the movement, on both its liberal and conservative wings, did recognize this connection.[77] But in general, the connection was not wanted. To have the movement labeled as "Hooverian" would amount to a political kiss of death.

VI

Over the course of sixty years, Herbert Hoover's historiographical fortunes have travelled a long and varied path. They have done so in part because of variations in the accessibility and scholarly use of primary materials. But also involved has been the impact of a changing society and changing political circumstances. The Great Depression, in particular, served both to expose New Era misperceptions and to generate new myths that met new political and social needs and were long accepted as historical reality. On the one hand, it punctured inflated pretensions of social progress, service-minded efficiency, and enlightened self-government. On the other, it created a historiographical cloud that obscured and distorted what had been valid about the perceptions of 1929, diverted historical study away from the Hoover years, and allowed the political caricatures of 1932 to gain and retain scholarly credence. Not until the late 1950s did the forces

"Herbert Hoover's Balanced Budget," *Wall Street Journal* (12 June 1980); and the commentary in McElvaine, *Great Depression*, 51-52.

[77]See Hawley, "'Industrial Policy' in the 1920s and 1930s;" Robert B. Reich, *The Next American Frontier* (New York: Times Books, 1983), chapter V; Linda L. Schuppener, "The Rehabilitation of the Corporatist Model," Ph.D. diss. (University of Iowa, 1987).

holding the cloud in place begin to weaken, thus permitting new perspectives on the period to develop and stimulate scholarly discoveries of a Hoover deeply engrossed in the problems of organizing and ordering a modern industrial society and modern international relations.

Was the newly discovered Hoover only another myth created in response to changing political circumstances and the emergence of new political and social needs? Some would argue that it was. And clearly, his emergence had coincided with the leftist search for weapons that could be used against liberal history, with a neo-libertarianism intent upon making departures from laissez-faire responsible for the Great Depression, with establishment attempts to find unity and continuity in the national past, and with new efforts to realize managerial ideals through non-statist institutions. Yet it was difficult to explain the revisionist triumphs entirely in terms of a new mythology being created by groups engaged in political and social struggle. They had also coincided with the recovery and documentation of historical behavior that diverged markedly from the type needed to sustain the interpretations found in either "liberal" or "conservative" history. The verified evidence to be interpreted had itself changed in dramatic fashion. And given this change, it seemed doubtful that the newly discovered Hoover would prove as unsubstantial as the one previously accepted by scholarly interpreters. If the long controversy over Hoover's place in modern history had not ended, it seemed at least to be entering a new phase characterized by a common acceptance of new evidence and a different set of competing perspectives.

In scholarly circles, then, the debate about Hoover that began in 1932 seemed to be ending. As of 1988, twenty-two years after the opening of the Hoover papers, the "new Hoover" of revisionist scholarship, about which new and different debates were underway, was becoming generally accepted. But the mythologies that had produced the older debate had proved strongly resistant to the new evidence and insights to be found in the scholarly works, and outside of scholarly circles the older images still enjoyed widespread credence.

Hoover and the Historians: The Reconstruction of a President

Patrick G. O'Brien
Philip T. Rosen

>This essay originally was published in three parts at different times in *The Annals of Iowa*. The first two segments appeared in Volume 46 (Summer and Fall 1981), and the final segment, prepared by Patrick G. O'Brien, appeared in Volume 49 (Summer 1988) under the title of "Hoover and the Historians: Revisionism Since 1980."

The most highly regarded man of his generation when elected president, Herbert Hoover was vilified when he left office. The public considered him aloof from the Great Depression that ravaged America, too inept and callous to generate economic recovery and provide relief to needy citizens. Historians contributed to Hoover's image as an irresponsible reactionary who lacked a sense of humanity. That image has gradually and largely been supplanted in historical writing as historians now often describe a humane reformer with an idealistic vision of America.

This essay has historiographical, bibliographical, and "editorial" dimensions.[1] It describes in general terms the

---

[1] An expansive and valuable bibliography in included in Joan Hoff Wilson, *Herbert Hoover: Forgotten Progressive* (Boston: Little, Brown, 1975), 284-300. Hoover receives only perfunctory attention in Donald R. McCoy, "Trends in Viewing Herbert Hoover, Franklin Delano Roosevelt, Harry S. Truman, and Dwight D. Eisenhower," *Midwest Quarterly* 29 (1979), 117-136. A substantive consideration of current literature is Robert H. Zieger, "Herbert Hoover: A Reinterpretation," *American Historical Review* 81 (1976), 800-810.

transition of the Hoover image in historical writing, identifies the pivotal contributors to the public and professional historical impressions of "the Chief" (a sobriquet acquired in his early mining career), and summarizes the influences on Hoover revisionism. This admittedly selective and cursory study is thereby an attempt to outline the fluid and complex contours of the historical writing on Hoover.

I

Herbert Hoover had one of the most interesting and productive backgrounds of any president. Exceptional ability, a prodigious capacity for work, and expansive interests enabled him to become a successful businessman in mining ventures on a global scale and among the most highly regarded public figures and humanitarians of his generation. Lionized as the secretary of commerce in the Warren G. Harding and Calvin Coolidge administrations, Hoover was a logical selection as the Republican presidential candidate in 1928.

Although Hoover was shy, his organization adeptly used the machinery of modern publicity to impress voters with his virtues in the 1928 presidential campaign. The hyperbolic 1928 campaign biographies presented Hoover as the new American folk hero. Will Irwin, newspaperman and friend of the next president, introduced the "log cabin" motif in *Herbert Hoover: A Reminiscent Biography*. As a descendent of solid colonial stock, Hoover was equated with Abraham Lincoln in that fate had chosen each of them to guide America. Ray Lyman Wilbur invoked the same analogy in his preface to Hoover's *The New Day: Campaign Speeches of 1928* when he compared the 1928 election with the cataclysmic 1860 election. In *The Presidency vs. Hoover*, Samuel Crowther described Hoover as a great organizer who fed "more human beings than any other man in history and has saved more lives." Crowther ascertained that stewardship, not politics, explained Hoover's activity in public life. Earl Reeves, in

This Man Hoover, concluded that "the Chief's" disregard of politics was his exemplary asset, and that the support for Hoover reflected a revolution in the society whereby administrators and efficiency experts would replace politicians. The 1928 campaign literature, which in summary presented Hoover as a disinterested and erudite public servant above politics, closely corresponded to the public impressions of him.[2]

The Great Depression brought Hoover into public disrepute, and strong expressions of defensiveness were present in the articles and books written in his behalf in the 1932 presidential campaign. As an example, Arthur Train compared Hoover's ordeal to those of George Washington, Thomas Jefferson, and Abraham Lincoln in *The Strange Attacks on Herbert Hoover*, and he accused the Hoover detractors of "malicious innuendo, deliberate false interpretations, and poisonous generalizations." In a more philosophical vein, Hugh A. Studdert Kennedy defined the persistence of individual liberty as the real campaign issue in *Hoover in 1932*, and ominously warned that "The day of principle is at hand."[3]

A few loyal and beleaguered defenders wrote in behalf of Hoover after his relegation to private life in the 1930s, but their influence on public opinion and the history profession was negligible. Of the several groups that supported Hoover, the most significant was composed of friends and public

---

[2]Samuel Crowther, *The Presidency vs. Hoover* (New York: Doubleday, Dorn, 1928) 126-127. See also William Hard, *Who's Hoover?* (New York: Dodd, Mead, 1928).

[3]Arthur Train, *The Strange Attacks on Herbert Hoover: A Current Example of What We Do to Our Presidents.* (New York: John Day, 1932), 5; Hugh A. Studdert Kennedy, . *Hoover in 1932.* (San Francisco, CA: Farrallon Press, 1932) v,3. On the 1932 campaign see also Herbert Hoover and Calvin Coolidge. *Campaign Speeches of 1932* (Garden City, NY: Doubleday, Doran, 1932); and Walter Friar Dexter, *Herbert Hoover and American Individualism: A Modern Interpretation of a National Ideal* (New York: Macmillian, 1932).

officials who had served under "the Chief" and published personal accounts and narratives to vindicate his policies and vision. William Starr Myers, an academician and friend, collected and edited *The State Papers and Other Public Writings of Herbert Hoover* in 1934. That same year, Hoover's press secretary Theodore G. Joslin published *Hoover Off the Record*. In 1936 Myers and Walter F. Newton, secretary to the president, authored *The Hoover Administration*. The next year, Arthur Mastick Hyde and Ray Lyman Wilbur, the former secretaries of agriculture and interior, contributed *The Hoover Policies*. These five writers postulated that "a fog of misrepresentation and calumny" obscured the Hoover years,[4] and they expressed faith that history would verify that Hoover, who had responded with originality and decisiveness to the Great Depression, was one of the ablest chief executives in modern American history.

In opposition to the small and uninfluential circle of defenders, the preponderance of polemicists, journalists, and historians zealously castigated Hoover. The acrimonious 1932 presidential election evoked a rash of malicious books. They agreed with each other that the president was a danger to the Republic, the premise in *Tough Luck: Hoover Again* by John C. Heaton. Representative "smear" biographies included Walter W. Liggett, *The Rise of Herbert Hoover*; Clement Wood, *Herbert Clark Hoover: An American Tragedy*; John Knox, *The Great Mistake*; and John Hamill, *The Strange Career of Mr. Hoover under Two Flags*. Hoover is variously described in these works as a misfit warped in childhood, a financial charlatan, and a perpetrator of slavery. "Never have so many written so much to besmirch one man," would be an apt paraphrase.

[4]The statement of Lewis Strauss is in Joseph Brandes, *Herbert Hoover and Economic Diplomacy: Department of Commerce Policy, 1921-1928* (Pittsburgh, PA: University of Pittsburgh Press, 1962), vii-viii. For an unusually objective view by a Hoover partisan see Joseph S. Davis, "Herbert Hoover, 1874-1964: Another Appraisal." *South Atlantic Quarterly* 67 (1969), 295-318.

Journalists and historians were usually more ethical and less histrionic than the authors of the smear biographies, but their equally uncomplimentary judgments of Hoover would be more cogent to the subsequent generation. The columnist Arthur Krock dismissed Hoover as an egregious failure as a party leader, economist, business authority, and personality. Allan Nevins completed the list of liabilities with his description of the president as an "exponent of narrow nationalism" and an inept political conservative. Hoover "botched the tariff, he botched farm relief, he botched prohibition—because he showed a Bourbon temper and an inelastic mind."[5]

These contemporary impressions of Hoover were transmitted and incorporated into the first generation of history. Ideologically liberal, politically partisan, and often personally influenced by the vicissitudes of the Great Depression, the bulk of historians reiterated and embellished the contemporary characterizations of Hoover in the 1940s and early 1950s. They were unimpressed with presidential policies; for example, Theodore Saloutos considered the Hoover farm program "a tragedy and a farce." Karl Schriftgiesser confidently repeated the previous prediction that "Hoover was to go down in history as the Great Failure" in *This Was Normalcy*. The history profession was basically united in its derogatory interpretation of Hoover.[6]

An exception to the pattern was an essay in *The American Political Tradition,* written by Richard Hofstadter and published in 1948. The low ebb of Hoover's reputation and the ideological lens of historians obscured the revisionist

---

[5]Arthur Krock, "President Hoover's Two Years." *Current History* 34 (1931), 494; Allan Nevins, "President Hoover's Record," *Current History* 36 (1932), 386-394.

[6]Theodore Saloutos, "William A Hirth: Middle Western Agrarian," *Mississippi Valley Historical Review* 38 (September 1951), 221; Karl Schriftgiesser, *This Was Normalcy: An Account of Party Politics During Twelve Republican Years, 1920-1932* (Boston: Little Brown, 1948), 264.

germ in the essay. In a somewhat vague and contradictory exposition, Hofstadter expressed a comprehension of Hoover's reputation that was unusual in the history profession and identified his neglected virtues. Hofstadter thought "There was nothing mythical about Hoover's vaunted ability;" stated that he had much in common with progressive premises and goals ("but he expected to reach it along the traditional highway"); allowed that Hoover opposed unregulated and predatory individualism; and concluded that Hoover's policies "did require a great deal more initiative than any president had ever brought to bear to meet a depression." The inference is that Hoover provided the groundwork for the New Deal.[7]

Hofstadter practiced the maxim of damn by faint praise. Acute personal and philosophical deficiencies nullified Hoover's merits; he represented the "last presidential spokesman of the hallowed doctrines of laissez-faire liberalism," and the "keynote" of his public life was "a return to the conditions, real or imagined of the past." Historians disregarded the revisionist possibilities in the Hofstadter essay and selectively adopted its conclusions that substantiated the political and ideological vices of Hoover.

The contribution of leftist historians such as Hofstadter to the resurrection of "the Chief" is an anomaly in Hoover historiography. When an allowance is made for leftist axioms and perspectives, their contribution to revisionism is explicable. The "old leftists" subscribed to the premises of traditional socialism or its derivatives. They considered capitalism of whatever form as invalid and its exponents of whatever ilk as misguided at best. The distinctions that liberal historians made between the New Era and the New Deal were largely inconsequential to the old left. Leftists could thereby practice "objectivity" toward Hoover in the

---

[7]Richard Hofstadter, "Herbert Hoover and the Crisis of American Individualism," in his *The American Political Tradition and the Men Who Made It* (New York: Knopf, 1948), 279-310.

sense that they were often equally harsh in their criticism, for example, of FDR and conscious of the affinity between Hoover and progressivism and the New Deal. Although the old leftists did not intend to raise the status of Hoover, their analysis could have contributed to it had the profession been conscious of the opportunity.

The preponderance of Americans acquired information about Hoover not from monographs, but through textbooks and professional perorations in the classroom. The textbook interpretations of Hoover ranged from highly critical through ambivalent to almost nonexistent. Samuel Eliot Morison and Henry Steele Commager were the authors of *The Growth of the American Republic*, which was among the most respected texts of its generation. It was generally derogatory of Hoover. The eager undergraduate reader was informed that Hoover was a capable food administrator, but a rugged individualist who adopted some "half-hearted" measures during the Great Depression. *Land of the Free* by Homer Carey Hockett and Arthur Meier Schlesinger complimented Hoover on his early public career, but stated that as president he was "faithful to his creed of rugged individualism" and adopted a few desultory policies during the economic conflagration. Hoover was nearly deleted from *The United States: From Wilderness to World Power* by Ralph Volney Harlow. The author compensated for the nearly studious neglect of Hoover with the generous statements that "President Hoover recommended an impressive program of public works to provide employment and to create a market for raw materials," and "For Latin America Roosevelt found the basis for a new policy already laid down by President Hoover." The bias of the history profession was transparent in most textbooks.[8]

---

[8]Samuel Eliot Morison and Henry Steele Commager, *The Growth of the American Republic*, 4th rev. ed., (New York: Oxford University Press, 1950); Homer Carey Hockett and Arthur Meier Schlesinger, *Land of the Free: A Short History of the American People* (New York: Macmillian, 1946); Ralph Volney Harlow, *The United States:*

The generally uncomplimentary characterizations of Hoover in textbooks and monographs were indicative of the low regard for "the Chief" within the historical circles. A small unscientific survey of historical opinion, published in 1948, described Hoover as just an average president in the twentieth position in the presidential hierarchy.[9] Although Hoover was rated higher than nine presidents of obviously dubious competence and integrity, he was included in the same categories with chief executives of the ilk of Chester Arthur. There was little to indicate that Hoover would be the subject of historical revisionism, but a confluence of circumstances would be responsible for a reexamination of Hoover and his administration.

The vehemence that most historians expressed toward Hoover was consistent with their "Progressive" interpretation of history. "Progressive" historians considered clashes of principle and philosophy between factions and classes endemic to the American past. They interpreted history in terms of conflict between selfless, idealistic reformers and selfish, predatory interests, usually business and its minions. Nearly all historians readily identified with the representatives of reform, and they were uninhibited about it in their writing. Fortuitous circumstances made it plausible for them to represent Hoover as the nemesis of democracy and economic justice and controversely to effuse over FDR and the New Deal.

A philosophical breach developed in the history profession when some practitioners began to expound the "Consensus" interpretation in the 1950s. The axiom of the

From Wilderness to World Power (New York: Henry Holt, 1949), vol. 2: 527, 267.

[9]Arthur M. Schlesinger, Sr., "Historians Rate the U.S. Presidents," *Life* 25 (1 November 1948), 65. Thomas A. Bailey, *Presidential Greatness: The Image and the Man from George Washington to the Present* (New York: Appleton-Century-Croft, 1966) is an interesting reference on the evaluation of presidents, and the Schlesinger surveys are considered on pages 23-34.

Consensus school was that Americans were united by principles that provided consistency in their past. Consensus and continuity, not conflict and disruption, were the realities of American history.[10] The "Consensus" historians often discerned merit in Hoover that had eluded their "Progressive" colleagues. That merit was usually that Hoover had ideological parallels with FDR and established precedents that would come to fruition in the New Deal. Hoover was thereby often considered in the New Deal context and not on his own terms.

The prognosis that Hoover's reputation would rise as the society became more conservative fails to explain the actual course of revisionism, Consensus historians were not perforce conservative, and many of them had marked political and ideological affinities with the Progressives. The static 1950s may have helped to impress historians with the veracity of Consensus, but their low opinion of Dwight D. Eisenhower as a passive-conservative president and symbol of the placidity of the era demonstrates that they did not discard their liberalism.[11] Although Hoover revisionism became respectable in the 1950s, the most original and provocative revisionism was not written in the "torpid fifties," but in a later era when Consensus was in eclipse. Consensus history may have been emphasized in the 1950s, but it was not the exclusive or even preponderant

[10]Louis Hartz, *The Liberal Tradition in America* (New York: Harcourt, Brace, 1955) is regarded as an exemplary "Consensus" statement. References on "Progressive" and "Consensus" history include John Higham, Leonard Krieger, and Felix Gilbert, *History* (Englewood Cliffs: Prentice-Hall, 1965); John Higham, ed., *The Reconstruction of American History* (New York: Humanities Press, 1962); Cushing Strout, *The Pragmatic Revolt in American History* (New Haven: Yale University Press, 1958); and John Higham, "Beyond Consensus: The Historian as Moral Critic," *American Historical Review* 67 (April 1962), 609-625.

[11]The 1962 Schlesinger poll rated Eisenhower as an average president and tied with Chester A. Arthur in twentieth position out of the twenty-nine presidents in the survey.

interpretation in the history profession, which is a confederation of methodological and philosophical factions. Both Progressive and Consensus interpretations were salient in historical writing during the 1950s.

Easily the most influential Progressive study of Hoover was by Arthur M. Schlesinger, Jr. He wrote in 1957 the "definitive" work on the Hoover era, *The Crisis of the Old Order, 1919-1933*, the first volume in the series on The Age of Roosevelt. Replete with epic form, impressive literary style, and footnotes, the book substantiated the Hoover stereotypes. FDR was the hero of the Great Depression, and Schlesinger used Hoover as a weak and archaic foil. The venial criticism of one reviewer that "with Roosevelt to explain is too often to condone; with Hoover to condemn" did not prevent Schlesinger from receiving the Francis Parkman Prize. The tendentious Harvard professor, attracted to activist Democrats of all generations, did not present an original explication of Hoover, but it was the most cogent scholarly indictment written of Hoover. Although even Schlesinger admitted that Hoover was not without compensatory virtues, he represented Hoover as a regressive president who by 1932 "moved from the New Era philosophy...toward something much closer to old-fashioned laissez-faire."[12] To have concluded otherwise would have, of course, nullified the Schlesinger thesis.

Although the strident Progressive interpretation of Hoover became less pronounced in the historical literature of the 1960s it was far from extinct. Editors Henry Steele Commager and Richard B. Morris report of Hoover in the introduction to *Republican Ascendancy, 1921-1933* that "not since the fateful decade of the 1850s had there been so egregious a failure of leadership in American politics." The

---

[12]Arthur M. Schlesinger Jr. *The Crisis of the Old Order, 1919-1933* (Boston: Houghton Mifflin, 1957), 235. See the review by Clarke A. Chambers in the *Mississippi Valley Historical Review* 44 (September 1957), 379-380.

book was a standard reference on the era. Its author, John D. Hicks, expressed the ambiance of the book in this representative passage:

> The leaders of business and industry were no longer content to have a politician in the White House who would do their bidding; they wanted a businessman as President, one who would instinctively reflect their every prejudice. In Hoover they had their ideal candidate.

Represented as an abject failure and flawed chief executive, Hoover could not be redeemed by the appreciable concession that he "made the nation's economic plight his concern to a degree that previous depression Presidents had never deemed necessary or feasible," and "In a sense the measures he ultimately felt obliged to support paved the way for the New Deal."[13]

Walter Johnson's *1600 Pennsylvania Avenue* profiled an intractable and inept chief executive who, through a myopic belief in the basic soundness of American capitalism, prolonged the Great Depression. Then Burl Noggle unabashedly pronounced in 1966 that "Hoover had little more depth than a Kiwanis Club noontime speaker." He also postulated that access to Hoover's papers would not change historical opinion.[14]

The more complimentary Consensus interpretations of Hoover gradually supplanted the tenacious Progressive stereotypes in the 1950s and 1960s. Although Consensus history often emphasized his virtues, academicians generally avoided the hyperbole of the sententious biographies of those decades and excessive reliance on Hoover's own *Memoirs*.[15]

---

[13]John D. Hicks, *Republican Ascendency, 1921-1933* (New York: Harper, 1960), xiii, 202, 234.

[14]Burl Noggle's review of Romasco, *Poverty of Abundance* in *Journal of American History* 52 (March 1966), 858-859.

[15]Examples of the effusive biographies that unconvincingly represented Hoover as one of the greatest men of the twentieth

The former president's three-volume autobiography, which was published in 1952, confirmed that he had never been his own most cogent defender. Although volume one of his *Memoirs*, which concluded with 1920, was generally well received by historians, the volumes on public office and the Great Depression were characterized by reviewers as bitter, inconsistent, and biased.

Hooverian foreign policy first attracted the interest of Consensus revisionists. In 1951 Alexander DeConde exploited a germ in previous literature to convincingly demonstrate that the FDR Good Neighbor Policy was firmly rooted in the Hoover administration. *Herbert Hoover's Latin American Policy* described the reorientation of United States policy through Hoover's visits to South American nations, mediation of disputes, and withdrawal of occupation troops from the region.[16] Richard N. Current contributed to the resurrection of Hoover when he contrasted the president's plan for peace with the secretary of state's policy of conflict in the explosive East Asian situation. Hoover was the definite "winner" over Henry L. Stimson in Current's comparative study. Robert H. Ferrell, *American Diplomacy in the Great Depression*, perceived Hoover as an able president who "represented some of the best informed thought of his time." He responded dramatically to the

---

century include Dorothy Horton McGee, *Herbert Hoover: Engineer, Humanitarian, Statesman* (New York: Dodd, Mead, 1959); Anne Emery, *American Friend: Herbert Hoover* (Chicago: Rand McNally, 1967); David Hinshaw, *Herbert Hoover: American Quaker* (New York: Farrar, Strauss & Young, 1950); James P. Terzian, *The Many Worlds of Herbert Hoover* (New York: Julian Messner, 1966); and Carol Green Wilson, *Herbert Hoover: A Challenge for Today* (New York: Evans, 1968).

[16] Alexander DeConde, *Herbert Hoover's Latin American Policy* (Stanford, CA: Stanford University Press, 1951). He somewhat revised his opinions in his review of Brandes, *Economic Diplomacy* in *American Historical Review* 68 (January 1963), 559.

economic cataclysm, but had "received no credit for his change of tactics toward the Depression."[17]

Revisionism on foreign policy had sufficiently grasped the history profession that by 1968 a reviewer omitted even a reference to the generally complimentary description of Hoover presented by L. Ethan Ellis in his highly regarded synthesis of *Republican Foreign Policy, 1921-1933*. The Republicans inherited a cycle of global turbulence, and Ellis concluded "that Republican leadership did achieve a considerable degree of adjustment to this new world." Ellis expressed a high regard for Hoover and, in particular, thought his foreign policy shift toward Latin America was "deliberate and positive," and his depression diplomacy was based upon "intelligent perception...and prompt action."[18]

Historians were more dilatory when it came to revision of Hoover's domestic career than they had been on foreign policy. It was in 1956 that Harold Wolfe published the revisionist biography *Herbert Hoover: Public Servant and Leader of the Loyal Opposition*. Although Wolfe admitted that "it is too early for a definitive biography to be written," he nevertheless established a strong revisionist precedent. He cited the impressive record of Hoover as secretary of commerce, including his promotion of commercial aviation and radio broadcasting. The two themes that became widely accepted in Consensus writing were graphically developed in the biography. Wolfe demonstrated first that Hoover actively intervened in the depression economy and second that many New Deal policies originated in the Hoover administration.

---

[17] Robert H. Ferrell, *American Diplomacy in the Great Depression: Hoover-Stimson Foreign Policy, 1929-1933* (New Haven, CT: Yale University Press, 1957), 10,15. Also see Richard N. Current, *Secretary Stimson: A Study in Statescraft* (New Brunswick: Rutgers University Press, 1954), and Alexander DeConde's review in the *Mississippi Valley Historical Review* 41 (September 1954), 360-361.

[18] L. Ethan Ellis, *Republican Foreign Policy, 1921-1933* (New Brunswick, NJ: Rutgers University Press, 1968), 367, 26.

Hoover revisionism was assisted by inquiry into his tenure as secretary of commerce. His contribution to conservation through the efficient and careful management of natural resources was emphasized by J. Leonard Bates in a 1957 article. A. Hunter Dupree identified Hoover as a technological progressive and administrator of research in *Science in the Federal Government*, which verified that he "was the one major political figure of the decade with an active appreciation of science."[19] In a monograph based upon the records of the Bureau of Foreign and Domestic Commerce, Joseph Brandes described the secretary as both a powerful policy maker and a "trouble-shooter for the Harding and Coolidge Administrations." A bold and able administrator, he was a bureaucratic imperialist who adopted an ambitious international program and "built the Department of Commerce into one of the most influential in the Federal Government."[20]

The disparate ideas of the revisionists were united into a comprehensive monograph in 1959. Convinced that historians had been unjust to Hoover, Harris Gaylord Warren's objective in *Herbert Hoover and the Great Depression* was to rectify that transgression. He stated unapologetically that Americans should be grateful that Hoover was president and that he was the "greatest Republican of his generation." An activist secretary of commerce, Hoover had a program more expansive than that of a chief executive. Unparalyzed by economic vicissitudes,

---

[19]J. Leonard Bates, "Fulfilling the American Democracy: The Conservation Movement, 1907-1921," *Mississippi Valley Historical Review* 44 (June 1957), 29-57; A. Hunter Dupree, *Science in the Federal Government* (Cambridge: Belknap Press, 1957), 338. Also see Rexmond C. Cochrane, *Measures for Progress: A History of the National Bureau of Standards* (Washington: U.S. Dept. of Commerce, 1966).

[20]Brandes, *Economic Diplomacy*, x, ix. Also see James H. Shindeler's review in the *Mississippi Valley Historical Review* 49 (March 1963), 729.

President Hoover was responsible for the precedent of strong federal government activity against the Depression. Besides regarding Hoover as the progenitor of the New Deal, Warren paid "the Chief" the dubious compliment that he played politics "with a skill worthy of Indiana's James E. Watson."[21]

An article by Carl N. Degler exemplified the revisionist current in the history profession and marked the furthest limit of the Consensus reexamination of Hoover. Well received and considered highly cogent in most history circles, the lucid Degler exposition had unusual influence for an essay. "The Ordeal of Herbert Hoover" in the *Yale Review* recognized his genuine progressivism and active economic intervention against the Great Depression. Degler also narrowed the gulf between Hoover and FDR: both were Wilsonians, accepted government intrusion in the economy, relied on World War I experience, and favored control of big business. Hoover was the transitory figure between the New Era and the New Deal, according to Degler.

Some historians synthesized the Consensus and Progressive interpretations. Although they acknowledged Hoover's unprecedented activism in the Great Depression, they usually regarded him as a poor politician with personality defects and ideological intractability. Albert Romasco, *The Poverty of Abundance*, was representative of this thesis. He refuted that Hoover was either an "ineffectual" or "weak President" and complimented him because he "was courageous enough to assume...leadership." Yet, the premises of Hoover's policies were archaic and even by his "new departure...was restricted by old ideas and old assumptions." "An idealist and conservative [Hoover] prepared the way for Franklin Delano Roosevelt and the New

[21]Warren, Harris G. *Herbert Hoover and the Great Depression* (New York: Oxford University Press, 1959), 24-32, 63-71. Warren relied upon Raymond Moley's characterization of Hoover in Moley, *Masters of Politics in a Personal Perspective* (New York: Funk & Wagnells, 1949), 28.

Deal: because he had failed" and "Hard experience taught...that new methods must now be tried."[22]

A randomly selected textbook off a library shelf documents both the diffusion of revisionism in the history profession and the impression that an undergraduate student would receive from assiduous study of class assignments. *The History of the United States*, written by Oscar Handlin, stated that in 1928 the Republicans nominated "Herbert Hoover, a Wilsonian who had earned a progressive reputation during the war and who campaigned as a forward-looking engineer able to solve the country's problem scientifically." Elected because of his "progressive record," Hoover was "determined to be a forceful and vigorous President." He "was not content to let the depression follow its own course," and "The failure of the economy to recover was not his fault." This description is in sharp contrast to the earlier textbook characterizations of Hoover and demonstrates how extensively some historians had modified their judgment of him.[23]

The revisionist influence did not, however, contribute appreciably to an increase of Hoover's status in the presidential hierarchy. In a 1962 survey, seventy-five respondents, including fifty-eight historians, classified twelve presidents as "average or mediocre." The rationale for classification indicates at least as much about the respondents as the presidents. Mediocre presidents "believed in negative government, in self-subordination to the legislative power. They were content to let well enough alone or, when not, were unwilling to fight for their programs or inept at doing so." Hoover was rated eighth among the mediocre

---

[22] Albert U. Romasco, *The Poverty of Abundance: Hoover, the Nation, the Depression* (New York: Oxford University Press, 1965), 9, 229, 232, 234. Also see William E. Leuchtenberg, *The Perils of Prosperity, 1914-1932* (Chicago: University of Chicago Press, 1958).

[23] Oscar Handlin, *The History of the United States* (New York: Holt, Rhinehart & Winston, 1968), vol. 2: 393-394, 418-419.

presidents. William McKinley, Rutherford B. Hayes, Martin Van Buren, and James Monroe eclipsed Hoover, who was designated nineteenth out of thirty-one presidents.[24]

An evaluation of presidents by historians that was published in 1970 indicated that Hoover was still regarded as weak, passive, inflexible, impractical, and unproductive. He was rated eighteenth of thirty-three presidents in "General Prestige," which represented an advance in the presidential hierarchy.[25] Hoover's glacial upward mobility in the polls indicated that revisionism had only faintly contributed to his resurrection among historians. The negligible influence of scholarship on professional historians provokes interesting conjecture about how they form and modify opinions. The low opinion of Hoover in the surveys arrested neither the interest nor the revisionist impulses toward him in the history profession.

A "Paradigm Shift," in the language of the advanced social sciences, is largely responsible for the present stage of Hoover revisionism that originated in about the middle 1960s. It is fairly easy to describe superficially the circumstances of the shift. The current generation of historians has a detachment toward Hoover that was impossible for their predecessors. Perspective has made them receptive to markedly different conclusions about Hoover than the historians who personally participated in the political dynamics that they studied and explicated. Historians now are not antiseptically neutral toward Hoover, but their writing often has the distinct advantage of reflection enabled only by time.

Although historians have the advantage of perspective, they are no less immune to presentism than the

---

[24] Arthur M. Schlesinger, Sr., "Our Presidents: A Rating by 75 Historians," *New York Times Magazine* (29 July 1962), 12.

[25] Gary M. Maranell, "The Evaluation of Presidents: An Extension of the Schlesinger Polls," *Journal of American History* 57 (June 1970), 104-113.

contemporaries of Hoover. The American panorama since World War II, especially the spasms of the Great Society, Vietnam, and Watergate, has aroused reservations about the New Deal precedents among historians of nearly all ideological hues. The scale and intensity of the disaffection cannot be stated with precision, but there are definite signs that New Dealism has waned in the history profession. This has enabled historians to discern previously unappreciated virtues in Hoover.

The premises of current and earlier Hoover revisionism often diverge. Consensus revisionism concentrated on the continuity between "the Chief" and the New Deal, and the resurrection of Hoover's reputation depended upon his identification as the progenitor of the New Deal and his affinity with FDR. Although the continuity thesis is highly visible in current historical writing, it often has a different emphasis than in the Consensus generation. This development combined with less fidelity to the New Deal has encouraged the study of Hoover on his own merits and in his own context, which has been fairer to Hoover and helpful to historical veracity. It is now even possible to consider Hoover's dissimilarity with FDR as a virtue.

An anomaly in the "paradigm shift" is that historians at the ideological poles have reversed themselves on Hoover. Whereas he was once anathema to the left and a paragon to the right, the opposite is now the case. The left and right generally agree in their description, but their opinions of him stem from divergent ideological postulates.

Libertarian Murray Rothbard is probably the most voluble and harshest critic of Hoover. He described Hoover as the activist instigator of the New Deal, which is the basis of his identification of Hoover as a protofascist. Hoover's presidential programs evolved logically from his secretariat. Government activism and intrusion in the society during the 1920s in the guise of Hooverian "voluntarism" was actually the "velvet glove of the mailed fist." All of Hoover's cooperative programs were predicated on government coercion should voluntarism fail. This background prepared Hoover to institute the "new economic science" in the Great Depression. Rothbard dismisses the 1933 "Roosevelt Revolution" as fiction because the New Deal originated in the 1929 "Hoover Revolution."[26]

The libertarian influence on Hoover historiography has been less pronounced than that of the New Left, which has been instrumental in the Hoover renascence. It has discerned character and vision in Hoover that eluded the "old left" and the bulk of the history profession. There is no ideological immunity to presentism, and the New Left has been influenced in its interpretations by the convulsions of society as well as dogma.

Hoover is the antithesis of the authoritarianism and duplicity of New Deal liberalism that the New Left imputes to government in the last generation. There are no precedents in the Hoover administration for the purported excesses of "imperial" presidents and unsavory government activities against dissidents and domestic radicals. Hoover himself was often the object, not the instigator of "dirty tricks." He warned Americans of the possible dangers of the welfare state in the New Deal form, and some members of the New Left have ascribed prophetic powers to him.

The New Left has even adduced at least faint parallels between the axioms of "participatory democracy" and "economic democracy" in the Hoover philosophy, but his foreign and military policy have especially elicited New Left

---

[26]See Rothbard, *America's Great Depression* (Princeton, NJ: D. Van Nostrand, 1963); "The Hoover Myth," *Studies on the Left* 4 (1966), 70-84; and contributions in Ellis W. Hawley et al., *Herbert Hoover and the Crisis of American Capitalism*, (Cambridge: Schenkman, 1973). Rothbard has relied heavily on the economist Benjamin M. Anderson, *Economics and the Public Welfare* (New York: D. Van Nostrand, 1949), 113-297.

approbation.[27] A virtual pacifist, Hoover opposed an extant military force capable of an offensive war, subscribed to disarmament, eschewed provocative policy, recoiled at the excesses of "economic imperialism" (including military intervention to protect American investments), and opposed a global crusade against Communism even in the most hyperbolic stage of the Cold War. Although historians need not be New Left to ascertain validity in Hoover's philosophy and policy, there is obviously much in them that is commendable to the New Left.

A seminal New Left contribution to Hoover revisionism was William Appleman Williams, *The Contours of American History*. It included a terse and thoughtful analysis of Hoover's economic and political theorems that verified his progressive and reform impulses and imputed the powers of a seer to him. Although Williams' conclusions would be disputed, his acute essay had a seismic influence on revisionism. It provided themes and perspectives that would be adopted, embellished, and often substantiated in later published works.

Williams lectured the history profession that:

> Hoover offers a classic example of the necessity for historians to break out of their own frame of reference if they are to understand the past. More than any other 20th-century American's, Hoover's reputation is the product of misinformation and distortion. He is also a notable example of the man whose ideas are borrowed by others without

---

[27]Selig Adler, "Hoover's Foreign Policy and the New Left," in M.L. Fausold and G.T. Mazuzan, eds. *The Hoover Presidency* (Albany: State University of New York Press, 1974), 153-163, criticizes New Left interpretations and accuses leftist historians of the rehabilitation of Hoover to detract from FDR. Joan Hoff Wilson, "Herbert Hoover Reassessed," in *Herbert Hoover Reassessed* (Washington, DC: GPO, 1981), 103-119, commends Hoover's opposition to "limitless open-ended" policies. On Hoover's attitudes toward the military see John Wilson, "The Quaker and the Sword: Herbert Hoover's Relations with the Military," *Military Affairs* 37 (1974), 41-47.

acknowledgement, and of the man whose analysis and insights are proved valid after an unfavorable stereotype has been established. For that reason it is easy to overlook them, and to assume that his failures comprise the whole story.[28]

In the vein of Polybius, Williams has unremittingly expounded the virtues of Hoover and the moral lessons to be drawn from his experience.

In conjunction with the "paradigm shift," accessibility to information has been responsible for the voluminous writing and influenced the nature of interpretations on Hoover. The Hoover Presidential Library in West Branch, Iowa opened in 1962 and admitted researchers four years later. Correspondence between revisionism and the availability of research collections is not just fortuitous as the presidential papers largely substantiate a favorable reconsideration of Hoover. The West Branch repository has enabled a profusion of studies on Hoover that would otherwise never have been written, and permitted historians to rely upon evidence rather than conjecture.

II

Almost every phase of Hoover's nature, life, and public career was reexamined in the 1970s. Historians nearly unanimously rejected the simplistic characterizations that once typified historical interpretation. Complex and multidimen-

---

[28]William Appleman Williams, "The Central Role of Herbert Hoover in the Maturation of an Industrial Gentry," in his *The Contours of American History* (Cleveland, OH: World, 1961), 426n. Also see Williams',"The Legend of Isolationism in the 1920's," *Science and Society* 18 (1954), 1-20; *Tragedy of American Diplomacy*, rev. ed., (New York: Dell, 1972); and his chapter on Hoover in *Some Presidents: Wilson to Nixon*, (New York: Vintage, 1972), ch. 2. Irwin Unger, "The New Left and American History: Some Recent Trends in United States Historiography," *American Historical Review* 72 (July 1967), 1237-1263, has some interesting impressions of the New Left.

sional, the Hoover in much revisionist writing is more of an enigma than before.

Although the subjects of Hoover's personality and ideology had been considered earlier, Hoover literature since 1970 is replete with commentary on references to his character and values. Gerald D. Nash identified "deep-seated beliefs regarding science and religion" as the foundations of Hoover's thought. A fusion of religious and scientific premises produced the themes of individualism, voluntary cooperation, and cooperative capitalism in Hoover's ideology. Nash thought that Quaker background likewise explained Hoover's behavior and habits. Simplicity, drabness, and sobriety were Quaker virtues, but these characteristics and a flawed personality contributed to Hoover's failure as a politician and thereby as president. "Highly efficient, rarely wrong in judgment, extremely ethical and benevolent, and the outstanding leader in every enterprise," was the magnanimous opinion that Hoover had of himself, according to Nash. That opinion was at variance with the reality of a fallible man of uneven effectiveness and faulty judgment in crises.[29]

Recent Hoover biographers Joan Hoff Wilson and David Burner modify and refine the Nash interpretation. Besides religion and science, both authors emphasize environment, including childhood vicissitudes and rural life, as a decisive influence on Hoover. They regard religion as a strong but residual influence. Wilson states that "as an adult Hoover retained few outward signs of his boyhood faith." He was a chronic smoker, fished on Sundays, liked a stiff drink, and swore—all practices inconsistent with Quakerism. These vices did not nullify his belief in basic Quaker postulates, and his idealism, stoicism, pragmatism, and social inhibitions

---

[29]Gerald D. Nash, essay in Hawley et al., *Herbert Hoover and the Crisis of American Capitalism*, 88, 93. Also see Geoffrey Blainey, "Herbert Hoover's Forgotten Years," *Business Archives and History* 3 (1963), 53-70.

likewise stemmed from his Quaker background. Burner especially regards Hoover as a complex person with highly divergent strains in his personality. His acute public shyness concealed his humor, sociability, and compassion, and his private inhibitions account for an elusiveness in his personality. Hoover could exhibit unattractive characteristics, but he was decent, humane, and honest. The high opinion that Hoover may have had of himself was usually merited.[30]

Able and ambitious, Hoover as a young man acquired a global reputation as a mining engineer and substantial wealth through business enterprises. To Edwin T. Layton in the effusively reviewed *The Revolt of the Engineers*, Hoover symbolized the emergence of the scientist and technician to status and influence in American society, and his activities "represented a large scale attempt to put into action some of the fundamental ideas of engineering thought."[31] Hoover had meshed science and public responsibility in his own thought, and he joined with like-minded associates to unite the engineering profession in behalf of social reform. The influence of the reform engineers reached its apex in the efficiency and planning philosophy of Hoover.

Hoover's compulsion for public service was fulfilled in World War I when he was responsible for Belgium relief, then appointed the U.S. administrator, and finally served as director of the American Relief Administration. His influence was imprinted on both wartime policy and the relief and reconstruction programs after the carnage. This phase of Hoover's career has attracted appreciable attention, and the nearly categorical opinion is that he was a highly successful

---

[30]Wilson, *Forgotten Progressive*, 4-7; David Burner, *Herbert Hoover: A Public Life* (New York: Knopf, 1978), x.

[31]Edwin T. Layton, *The Revolt of the Engineers: Social Responsibility and American Engineering Profession* (Cleveland: Press of Case Western Reserve University, 1971), 226. Also see John B. Rae, "Memorial for Herbert C. Hoover," *Technology and Culture* 6 (1965),108-109.

administrator whose policies compatibly fused American self-interest and humanitarianism.[32]

Early in his government tenure, Hoover displayed an administrative style that continued through his presidency. The premise of *Aggressive Introvert* by Craig Lloyd is that Hoover's personal shyness prescribed his administrative methods. Hoover preferred to work "through figureheads, committees, conferences, and the printed media." The system insulated the shy Hoover and enabled his centralized control of activities to educate the public in civic responsibility. The system worked until the Great Depression when it contributed substantially to Hoover's failure.[33]

The 1918 to 1921 interim was pivotal to the crystallization of Hoover's ideology and included the prerequisite political groundwork for the presidency. Astringent and conscientiously researched, *The Politics of American Individualism* by Gary Dean Best is the standard monograph on the Hoover ideological and political odyssey from the

---

[32]Hoover's tenure as food administrator is examined in Witold S. Sworakowski, "Herbert Hoover, Launching the American Food Administration." in L.E. Gelfand, ed. *Herbert Hoover, Great War and Its Aftermath* (Iowa City: University of Iowa Press, 1979), 40-60, and Donald D. Winters, "The Hoover-Wallace Controversy During World War I," *Annals of Iowa* 39 (1969), 586-597. His post-war policies have been popular subjects in the last decade, see Gary Dean Best, "Herbert Hoover's Technical Mission to Yugoslavia, 1919-1920," *Annals of Iowa* 42 (1974), 443-459; Best, "Food Relief as Price Support: Hoover and American Pork, January-March 1919," *Agricultural History* 45 (1971), 49-84; Murray N. Rothbard, "Hoover's 1919 Food Diplomacy in Retrospect," in Gelfand, ed., *Great War*, 87-110; and Robert H. Van Meter, Jr., "Herbert Hoover and the Economic Reconstruction of Europe," in Gelfand, ed., *Great War*, 143-181.

[33]Hoover's administrative style has also been discussed in Robert D. Cuff, "Herbert Hoover, the Ideology of Voluntarism and War Organization During the Great War," *Journal of American History* 64 (1977), 358-372. Reprinted in Gelfand, ed., *Great War*, Cuff states that Hoover's reliance on voluntarism was a tool of political manipulation, bureaucratic control, and evasion of accountability.

armistice to the secretaryship. Identified as a progressive and internationalist, he was the choice of many Republicans and Democrats as a presidential candidate. Robert F. Himmelberg explains that Hoover's popularity stemmed from his media images of competence, justice, and reason that appealed to an American society that was convulsed by divisiveness and repression. Although rebuffed as a Republican candidate, Hoover demonstrated a strong political base and erudition that enabled his admission to the cabinet.[34]

The fruition of his ideological introspection from 1918 to 1921 was "American Individualism," unfortunate terminology that contributed to the impression that it was "rugged individualism." George H. Nash discerns "the roots of Herbert Hoover's philosophy in the contrast he perceived between the Old World and the New."[35] His vision was an American society with equal opportunity, the mesh of individualism and social responsibility, the absence of classes and class consciousness, and the practice of cooperation without the loss of constructive competition. With these multiple, complex, and close to contradictory veins in Hoover's ideology, it is easy to understand why it is subject to a profusion of interpretations and why Hoover evades simple political taxonomy. It is now the conventional interpretation that Hoover was a progressive, but there were

---

[34]Robert F. Himmelberg, "Hoover's Public Image, 1919-1920: The Emergence of a Public Figure and a Sign of the Times," in Gelfand, ed., *Great War*, 207-232. Hoover's progressive reputation stemmed largely from his attitudes toward labor, see Gary Dean Best, "President Wilson's Second Industrial Conference," *Labor History* 16 (1975), 505-520. Hoover supported the Versailles Treaty with reservations, see Royal J. Schmidt, "Hoover's Reflections on the Versailles Treaty," in Gelfand, ed., *Great War*, 61-86. Best, "The Hoover-for-President Boom of 1920," *Mid-America* 53 (1971), 227-244, is useful on presidential politics.

[35]George H. Nash, "The Social Philosophy of Herbert Hoover," *Annals of Iowa* 45 (1980), 496.

infinite species of progressivism and the generic label does little to explain his ideology.[36]

Historians have increasingly relied upon Ellis W. Hawley's interpretations of the "associative state" to explain Hoover's ideological vision and guide to his policies. The idealistic, practical, and complex Hoover had a comprehensive plan to adapt American society to the twentieth century without the loss of past values. He zealously assisted cooperative institutions to form a type of private government that would "preserve and work through individual units, committing them voluntarily to service, efficiency, and ethical behavior." His construction of networks, organization of constituencies, and voluminous programs of education and publicity were his administrative and political mechanisms to implant the "associative state."[37]

Revisionism of the past decade has confirmed and expanded upon the Consensus era literature of Hoover as a reform and activist secretary of commerce. It has also refuted Hoover mythology and expressed greater comprehension of his vision. The preponderance of historians agree with Robert H. Zieger that Hoover "formulated a bold analysis of American capitalism from the variegated strands of prewar

---

[36]Himmelberg's essay in Hawley et al., *Herbert Hoover and the Crisis of American Capitalism*, examines Hoover's ideology and policy on control and concludes that he was in the New Freedom progressive school. David Burner and Thomas R. West broaden the consideration of Hoover, a progressive and later a conservative in American lexicon, "to see what he looks like against a background of philosophically stronger conservative and traditionalist concerns elaborated in western thought" (p.236). Their conclusion in "Technocrat's Morality: Conservativism and Hoover the Engineer," in Stanley Elkins and Eric Mekitrick, eds. *The Hofstadter Aegis: A Memorial* (New York: Alfred A. Knopf, 1974) is that his affinity with many conservative postulates fails to make him an archetypical conservative.

[37]Hawley, "Herbert Hoover, the Commerce Secretariat, and the Vision of an 'Associative State,' 1921-1928," *The Journal of American History* 41 (June ,1974), 117.

progressivism" and "his ideas still stand as a monument to the continuity of progressivism through the 1920s."[38]

The derogatory Progressive interpretation of Hoover stemmed from the belief that he defended business interests to the exclusion of labor and agriculture. Hoover revisionism has now cogently refuted that Progressive staple. Robert H. Zieger concentrates on the neglected topic of *Republicans and Labor, 1919-1929*. The secretary of commerce was an influential instigator of labor policy and representative of labor welfare in Republican administrations. He "worked constantly to mute labor-management antagonism and to reduce the waste and disruption that both caused and grew from labor troubles," and his objective to "create a whole pattern of labor relations based on concepts of efficiency and cooperation" attracted reformers and unionists.[39] Zieger expands upon Hoover's labor philosophy and practices in subsequent articles, which are unequivocal statements of Hoover's genuine concern for labor and his acceptance of collective bargaining and other measures to increase real wages, raise the standard of living, and advance "welfare capitalism."

The writing on Hoover's attitudes and policies toward agriculture has been as revisionist as that on labor. Joan Hoff Wilson, in "Hoover's Agricultural Policies, 1921-1928," describes Secretary Hoover's ideas on agriculture as original, compliments his "comprehensive view" of the farm problem, and dismisses as "patently false" the accusation that Hoover sacrificed the farmer to big business. Gary H. Koerselman concludes that Hoover had more genuine concern for the "dirt farmer" than many agrarian representatives. In the

---

[38]Robert H. Zieger, "Labor, Progressivism, and Herbert Hoover in the 1920's," *Wisconsin Magazine of History* 58 (1975), 196-208.

[39]Zieger, *Republicans and Labor, 1919-1929* (Lexington: University of Kentucky Press, 1969), 13. Also see his essay, "Herbert Hoover, the Wage Earner, and the 'New Economic System,' 1919-1929," *Business History Review* 51 (1977), 161-189.

assignment of responsibility for the economic hardships of the farmer, he states that the "agricultural leaders themselves must shoulder most of the blame...."[40]

The manifold economic activities of the secretary had prosperity for the whole society as an objective. In "Secretary Hoover and the Emergence of Macroeconomic Management," Evan B. Metcalf describes Hoover's amplification of government responsibility to provide full employment through stabilization of business production and investment. His success in mitigation of seasonal and minor cyclical fluctuations explains his original reliance on business initiative in the Great Depression and anticipated official government policies to manage prosperity.[41]

Only a few books in the last decade have surveyed the Hoover administration. Written for the general public, Gene Smith, *The Shattered Dream*, had little value to professional historians. Edgar Eugene Robinson and Vaughn Davis Bornet, *Herbert Hoover*, was afflicted by fuzzy prose, a patent Hoover bias, and neglect of pivotal Hoover scholarship. Although not uniformly informative and cogent, the essays that comprised Martin L. Fausold and George T. Mazuzan (eds.), *The Hoover Presidency* attained an unusually high level for an anthology.

The Great Depression is the valid focus of the Hoover administration, but it has been considered to the exclusion of his pre-Depression contributions. David Burner rectified the omission first in an essay in *The Hoover Presidency* and then in his biography of "the Chief." He describes an activist president responsible for genuine reforms in civil rights, prisons, Indian affairs, child welfare, and conservation. J.

---

[40] Gary H. Koerselman, "Secretary Hoover and National Farm Policy: Problems of Leadership," *Agricultural History* 51 (1977), 395.

[41] A discrete study that confirms Hoover's macroeconomic responsibility of government is Carolyn Grin, "The Unemployment Conference of 1921: An Experiment in National Cooperative Planning," *Mid-America* 55 (1973), 83-107.

Richard Snyder supplements Burner's conclusions on the pre-Depression presidency. The political ineptitude thought to be characteristic of Hoover is refuted in his study on the widely miscomprehended politics of the Hawley-Smoot Tariff. Hoover's "legislative leadership" on this complex and divisive issue is summarized as "impeccable."

The Depression phase of the presidency explicably received the most attention by historians. Although not stated with the vehemence of the first generation historians, there is still a residue of acrimony in the Hoover literature. An unusual concession in Jordan A. Schwarz, *The Interregnum of Despair*, is that Hoover "had some continuity with the New Deal." Apprehensive of government reform and activism, Hoover acquiesced to new departures while "Congress...became the reluctant vehicle for an orderly and coherent transmogrification in the relationship between the federal government and the economy."[42] This originally harsh judgement was compounded when Schwarz examined the bases of antipathy between Hoover and Congress in an essay in *The Hoover Presidency*, which castigated Hoover for political incompetence, egregious flaws in temperament, contempt for elected officials, and dogmatic ideas on government responsibility and the congressional role in government.

Ellis W. Hawley is more representative of historical opinion. He states that Hoover had an activist antidepression program, but that he was unwilling to adopt measures incompatible with his ideology. Committed to his inviolate blue print, Hoover consigned himself to public ignominy rather than modify it. Hawley's most comprehensive statement of the theme is *The Great War and the Search for Modern Order*, which includes the "story of the Hoover vision at bay, of an administration still committed to the formulas of 1929, fighting desperately...to restore faith

---

[42]Jordan A. Schwarz, *Interregnum of Despair: Hoover, Congress, and the Depession* (Urbana: University of Illinois Press, 1970), vii.

in them and to block what it considered prescriptions for bureaucratic despotism and social degeneration."[43] Yet Hawley discerns idealism, validity, and continuity with the New Deal in Hoover's ideology.

Historians increasingly defend Hoover in the Depression phase. An example is Barry D. Karl's "Presidential Planning and Social Science Research: Mr. Hoover's Experts." Not only does it dispel the mythology of Hoover inactivity during an economic cataclysm, but the "American revolutionary" continued to expound "social science utopianism" and work toward a "Great Society." Unprecedented is James Stuart Olson's impression of Hoover's depression policies in *Herbert Hoover and the Reconstruction Finance Corporation, 1931-1933*. In refutation of the paralysis, callousness, and dogmatism imputed to Hoover, Olson is emphatic that Hoover transcended ideological inhibitions to his antidepression measures. The failure of his programs to arrest the downward economic spiral cannot be ascribed to the litany of Hoover's deficiencies in Schwarz. The continuity that Olson perceives between Hoover and the New Deal is both in the unduplicated use of government and concrete administrative and legislative measures. Hoover "should not be remembered as the man who followed Calvin Coolidge in the White House, but as the man who preceded Franklin Roosevelt."[44]

---

[43]Ellis W. Hawley, *The Great War and the Search for Modern Order, A History of the American People and Their Institutions, 1917-1933* (New York: St. Martin's, 1979), 193. Also see his essay "Herbert Hoover and the American Corporatism, 1929-1933," in Fausold and Martin, eds., *The Hoover Presidency*. An earlier failure in associationism is examined by Hawley in "Secretary Hoover and the Bituminious Coal Problem, 1921-28," *Business History Review* 42 (1968), 247-270. Martin L. Fausold, "President Hoover's Farm Policies, 1929-1933," *Agricultural History* 51 (1977), 362-377, concludes that the Hawley thesis is applicable to Hoover's farm policies, but only that it might be valid in other policy fields.

[44]James Stuart Olson, *Herbert Hoover and the Reconstruction Finance Corporation, 1931-1933* (Ames: Iowa State University

Of the many failures imputed to Hoover in the presidency, his alleged callousness toward unemployed, dispirited, and indigent citizens was considered his most reprehensible transgression. Even those detractors willing to excuse Hoover's inability to generate economic recovery could not excuse his supposed inhumanity to Americans in desperate need. It is now well known that Hoover had genuine concern for citizens in penurious circumstances, and revisionist historians have defended his relief programs as unprecedented. Hoover's attitudes and policies on relief are not immune to criticism, but he cannot be reproached as malicious.[45]

The Bonus March and subsequent Riot confirmed Hoover's worst frailties to many Americans and historians. Donald J. Lisio expunges misunderstanding in the thoroughly researched and well written monograph entitled *The President and Protest: Hoover, Conspiracy, and the Bonus Riot.* Sympathetic to veterans and the author of the reform programs in their behalf, Hoover provided the bonus marchers with supplies and shelter, defended their civil liberties, and worked to avoid violence. An important Lisio contribution is his incontrovertible documentation that General Douglas MacArthur disobeyed Hoover's order when he routed the veterans. Hoover may have been culpable of

---

Press, 1977), 90. On the deficiencies of the RFC and Hoover's response to the Depression, also see Olson's "Rehearsal for Disaster: Hoover, the RFC, and the Banking Crisis in Nevada, 1932-1933," *Western Historical Quarterly* 6 (1975), 149-161; and "The End of Voluntarism: Herbert Hoover and the National Credit Association," *Annals of Iowa* 41 (1972), 1104-1113. Olson attempts to demonstrate that Hoover's philosophy is more germane in this generation than during his presidency in "The Philosophy of Herbert Hoover: A Contemporary Perspective," *Annals of Iowa* 43 (1976), 181-191.

[45]See Roger C. Lambert, "Hoover, Red Cross and Food for the Hungry," *Annals of Iowa* 44 (1979), 530-540; Richard T. Ortquist, "Unemployment and Relief: Michigan's Response to the Depression During the Hoover Years," *Michigan History* 57 (1973), 209-236.

poor communications, political misjudgment, and unmerited loyalty to a subordinate, but not inhumanity and repression.[46]

The early Consensus attention to Hooverian foreign policy may explain why the bulk of historical writing in the last decade has been on domestic policy. Yet, historians have not neglected foreign policy. A revisionist Hoover is ubiquitous in Joan Hoff Wilson's *American Business and Foreign Policy, 1920-1933*. The complementary veins of practicality and idealism in Hoover were evident in his foreign policy principles, which usually were attuned to the realities of the post-war world. Wilson neglects neither the inconsistencies nor the myopia in Hoover's global vision, but she implores readers to appreciate his valid contributions and apply them to the present. Her conclusions on Hoover are representative interpretations in much historical writing.[47]

Although the favorable impression of his foreign policy that originated in the Consensus era has continued to the present, contemporary literature includes both ambivalence toward and rebuke of Hoover. Richard N. Kottman concluded in his study of the complex diplomacy of the St. Lawrence Seaway Treaty that "Hoover was too often politically inept, too vindictive, too irascible and suspicious, too sensitive to criticism, too dogmatic...and too rigid." But "at the same time [he] manifested vision, occasional political courage, and a determined commitment to effecting a great

---

[46]Donald J. Lisio, *The President and Protest: Hoover, Conspiracy, and the Bonus Riot* (Columbia: University of Missouri Press, 1974). A divergent interpretation that also absolves Hoover of complicity in the rout is Roger Daniels, *The Bonus March: An Episode of the Great Depression* (Westport, CT: Greenwood Press, 1971).

[47]Joan Hoff Wilson, *American Business and Foreign Policy, 1920-1933* (Lexington: University of Kentucky Press, 1971). Also see Frank Costigliola, "The Other Side of Isolationism: The Establishment of the First World Bank, 1929-1930," *Journal of American History* 59 (1972), 602-620; Melvin Leffler, "The Origins of Republican War Debt Policy, 1921-1933: A Case Study in the Applicability of the Open Door Interpretation," *Journal of American History* 59 (1972), 585-601.

national enterprise." In "Herbert Hoover and the Smoot-Hawley Tariff: Canada, A Case Study," the same author discerned less to commend in the president, and concluded with a testy challenge to the revisionists that they "will have a difficult task to reconcile this 'new Hoover' with the realities of Canadian-American relations, 1929-1933."[48]

Hoover's post-presidential years have not received the studious attention that historians applied to his prior public career. Except for his assignments in the Harry S Truman administration and work in the Hoover commissions, this phase of his life has been neglected. With the exceptions noted above, extant studies usually emphasize his choleric dissent from the course of history in general and the New Deal in particular. It is easy to understand how Hoover could be dismissed as a bitter anachronism. His intemperate language and rhetorical excesses made it appear that he was engaged in a vendetta brought on by frustration and rebuff. It can be said in Hoover's defense that his political opponents, ideological nemeses, and American public usually heard only what they wanted.

Gary Dean Best focuses upon Hoover's disaffection with the New Deal. Although Hoover first avoided publicity as a private citizen, he was resolved to be the titular head of the Republican party. Not especially effective in his objectives to encourage Republican public opposition to the New Deal and shape the party into a vehicle of alternatives to it, Hoover renounced "public silence and private anguish" to become a strident detractor of the domestic New Deal. Hoover then transferred his dissent to foreign policy. Revulsion toward war, antipathy toward both Communism and Fascism, and fear of domestic regimentation explain his futile protest

---

[48]Richard N. Kottman, "Herbert Hoover and the St. Lawrence Seaway Treaty of 1932," *New York History* 56 (1975), 315; "Herbert Hoover and the Smoot-Hawley Tariff: Canada, A Case Study," *Journal of American History* 62 (1975), 635. Also critical is his study of "The Hoover-Bennett Meeting of 1931: Mismanaged Summitry," *Annals of Iowa* 42 (1974), 205-221.

against World War II interventionist policy. He misjudged the Nazi military capacity and the effect of war on society, but his comprehension of geopolitics and the consequences of the war on the global power system surpassed that of the FDR administration.[49]

World War II did not appreciably modify Hoover's perceptions. Afterward, he became a vehement critic of Truman's foreign policy because of international alliances and domestic mobilization that resulted in the "military-industrial complex." Donald J. Mrozek states that Hoover's "special definition of American individualism...forced him to oppose Truman's policy," not misguided isolationism as his opponents thought. The Truman policy "endangered the possibilities for imperial growth within the domestic limits of constitution and tradition."[50]

The conclusion should not be drawn from the above description that Hoover was either immune to ideas not his own or incapable of adaptation to new realities. As the influential chairman of the First Hoover Commission, he contributed to bipartisan acceptance of the strong managerial executive, a New Deal axiom. Convinced that the authority of the office must be equivalent to its official responsibility and based upon strictly managerial terms, Hoover was less willing than commission liberals to confine the presidency to an organizational form.[51]

The profusion of monographs on disparate phases of Hoover's life and political career was synthesized into two revisionist biographies published in the latter stages of the

[49]See Gary Dean Best, "Herbert Hoover as Titular Leader of the GOP, 1933-1935," *Mid-America* 61 (1979), 81-97; "Totalitarianism or Peace: Herbert Hoover and the Road to War, 1939-1941," *Annals of Iowa* 44 (1977), 516-529.

[50]Donald J. Mrozek, "Progressive Dissenter: Herbert Hoover's Opposition to Truman's Overseas Military Police," *Annals of Iowa* 43 (1976), 275-291.

[51]Peri E. Arnold, "The FirstHoover Commission and the Managerial Presidency," *Journal of Politics* 38 (1976), 46-70.

1970s. Joan Hoff Wilson, *Herbert Hoover: Forgotten Progressive*, and David Burner, *Herbert Hoover: A Public Life*, have parallel themes and conclusions. The divergence between them is less in interpretation than in emphasis, style, and attitude. Wilson's characterization of Hoover as a *Forgotten Progressive* indicates both the premises and the cogency of current revisionism on Hoover. The occasionally obtuse style, expression of "presentism," and intermittently metallic criticism of Hoover fail to invalidate the scholarship in *Forgotten Progressive*. *A Public Life* has all the merits and few of the liabilities of *Forgotten Progressive*, and it is the best one volume biography extant.

III

Assiduously "bashed" by progressive historians, Herbert Hoover suffered a generation of infamy as a callous and inept reactionary. Writing from widely varied viewpoints, revisionists convincingly resurrected "the Chief" from progressive ignominy between the late 1950s and about 1980. Progressive and revisionist versions of Hoover had slight resemblance. Historians of the progressive variety claimed to be unaware that Hoover had redeeming qualities. Revisionists, however, revealed the reform efforts, decent impulses, and broad vision of the less-than-perfect "Chief," and some even certified that he was a New Dealer.

Immutable historical interpretation is as common as a vacuum in nature, so it is not surprising that many of the impressions of Hoover in historical writing since 1980 diverge from those during the apogee of revisionism. Although Hoover literature since the 1950s cannot be neatly divided into inviolate phases, a perceivable transition between "initial" and "derivative" revisionism occurred early in this decade. Writing after 1980 can largely be construed as derivative in the sense that it has generously and explicably appropriated many ideas and concepts of earlier revisionism. Dissimilarity between the phases is, however, as evident as continuity. Although a portion of later writing may not equal the verve of initial revisionism, it is emphatically not without significant qualities. Later writing has encompassed new topics, applied twists to old ones, and even added facets to the already complex and enigmatic "Chief." One of the biggest differences in revisionism before and after 1980 is that the latter often has a harsher tone and less flattering assessments of Hoover.

Herbert Hoover Reassessed: Essays Commemorating the Fiftieth Anniversary of the Inauguration of Our Thirty-First President may represent the high point and fruition of initial revisionism.[52] A sprawling anthology of twenty-nine essays with pronounced unevenness, the contributors largely restate their earlier and complimentary interpretations of "the Chief." Originality is neither expected nor particularly evident in this commemorative volume, but it is a useful summary and gauge of initial revisionist interpretations and sentiments.

Not all books, of course, have been inordinately negative toward Hoover, and that is especially the case with one that closed a huge biographical gap. Any neglect and superficiality with regard to Hoover's life and career before entry into public service is rectified in George H. Nash, *The Life of Herbert Hoover: The Engineer, 1874-1914*.[53] This exemplary first book in a projected multi-volume biography is exhaustively researched, cogently written, and jammed with keen analysis. Although earlier revisionist influences are apparent, Nash's analysis is singular.

A terse review of Hoover's family history and childhood has incisive commentary on his personality, particularly as a consequence of his parents' deaths and unsatisfactory surrogates. Described in unequivocal terms is the Stanford

---

[52] *Herbert Hoover Reassessed: Essays Commemorating the Fiftieth Anniversary of the Inauguration of Our Thirty-First President* (Washington, DC: GPO, 1981).

[53] Nash, George H., *The Life of Herbert Hoover: The Engineer, 1874-1914* (New York: W.W. Norton, 1983).

influence on Hoover, and his inviolate attachment to the institution that substituted as family and home, provided his future wife, and prepared him for a career. The last is the book's emphasis, and it is absorbing biography, as well as economic, business, and social history, often on a global scale. Compulsively ambitious, calculating and astute, and inhumanly stubborn, Hoover's business failures and career frustrations were minimal when compared with his phenomenal success. Not above shrewd dealing and self-aggrandizement, he was fundamentally principled and decent, which made him somewhat conspicuous in mining and financial circles.

Nash is persuasive on the proposition that Hoover's later policies reflected views formulated while a private citizen involved with public issues. With an "aggressive introvert" personality, his instinct for unobtrusive control was sharpened by the machinations of international business, finance, and politics. "The Chief" would certainly squirm, stew, and erupt at portions of this book, but it is a model of critical and sympathetic biography.

Hoover's secretariat and presidency naturally elict the greatest interest, provoke the widest controversy, and clearly reflect the trend toward less generous appraisals. Although each writer may adduce specific reasons to reprove Hoover, they are part of a larger framework in a sequence of perceptions. Restrained criticism of the initial revisionists was generally within the limits of new perceptions of "the Chief" as either an incipient New Dealer or exponent of "associative state" voluntarism and cooperation, which allowed government guidance with a modicum of coercion. Although these were not wholly compatible views, both nullified the progressive caricature of a nineteenth century *laissez-faire*, individualistic reactionary with an unabashed business bias and veneration of competition. Hoover's resurrection to respectability was perhaps based more on what he was not than what he was. This favorable shift in perception, however, failed to cloak "the Chief" with immunity.

Hoover has been a vulnerable target in this decade, and it is tied in part to the issue of the New Era as prologue to the New Deal. Whereas initial revisionists often discerned strong continuity between the two, later writers are prone to regard it as more tenuous. Although "the Chief's" critics readily admit that his philosophy and policies were not of the antediluvian sort perceived by progressive historians, they often echo the progressive critique when they assert that they may as well have been when judged by the consequences.

Hoover's beliefs and programs, now largely equated with those of the associative state, have been subjected to a review probably more exacting and comprehensive than those of any other public figure. Often short on generosity, many historians have dismissed his blueprint and policies as inadequate to the realities of the 1920s and exigencies of the Great Depression. Evidence that Hoover used new departures to sustain prosperity in the expansive 1920s and resorted to unprecedented measures to generate economic recovery in the convulsions of the Great Depression satisfied many early revisionists, but later writers have judged Hoover less by his vision and goals than by their results.

Hoover's sagging reputation has partially turned on his limited and tentative recourse to government intervention as secretary of commerce and president. That issue, however, is not solely responsible for his limited eclipse. His political acumen, personality, administrative style, and social convictions have often generated equal controversy, and some have ignored no opportunity to emphasize his purported or genuine weaknesses. Even those basically sympathetic toward Hoover often discern less than admirable qualities that the initial revisionists overlooked or of which they were unaware.

Still unexplained is where Hoover found the necessary energy and mental concentration for his multifarious projects as secretary of commerce. Between 1921 and 1928 he gave full rein to his associative state reform impulses that ranged from the attempted rescue of struggling industries to improving the health care afforded children. Virtually without exception, historical writing since 1980 approves of Hoover's ideals and objectives.

Yet conclusions in the same writing by and large contradict the earlier favorable revisionist assessment that contributed to "the Chief's" resurrection. Not transfixed by his secretariat record, later writers emphasize its shortcomings. They would claim that his liabilities as president reflect those as secretary and were predictable. Impressions of Hoover in the two offices are actually almost inverted in the writing after 1980 in the sense that he is presented as more willing as chief executive to modify stifling principles than while running his secretariat A consequence of the downgrading of Hoover as secretary is by comparison to raise his evaluation as president, which is definitely faint consolation.

Typical praise is bestowed on Hoover's perspicacity and goals in William J. Barber, *From New Era to New Deal: Herbert Hoover, the Economists, and American Economic Policy, 1921-1933*.[54] No person was more convinced of the validity and more influential and assiduous in the promotion of New Era propositions like high wages than Hoover. Committed to a rational, productive, and humane economy, he was as aware of the keys to national income and employment as anyone in his generation and as willing to use government in pursuit of prosperity. Barber's broad and coherent context is helpful in defining the roles of specific policies in Hoover's macroeconomic scheme. Not all of Barber's content is new, but it is readable and instructive economic history that cogently argues that Hoover's views

---

[54]Barber, William J., *From New Era to New Deal: Herbert Hoover, the Economists, and American Economic Policy, 1921-1933* (New York: Cambridge University Press, 1985).

were profoundly advanced when compared with contemporaries.

A collection of uniformly impressive essays, first presented at the Herbert Hoover Centennial Seminars, is contained in Ellis W. Hawley, ed., *Herbert Hoover as Secretary of Commerce: Studies in New Era Thought and Practice*.[55] The Hoover secretariat is also the subject of essays in Carl E. Krog and William R. Tanner, eds., *Herbert Hoover and the Republican Era: A Reconsideration*.[56] A composite Hoover is not easily assembled from the disparate topics and perspectives in these anthologies, but they basically portray an activist and rational manager with an associative state reform blueprint compounded of realism and idealism. Although the Hoover reform view was never starkly economic, nearly all of the essays in these anthologies deal with his economic policies and theories. Generally described in the essays is not the archetypical reactionary of progressive animus, but a secretary committed to the welfare of farmers and workers, interested in industrial democracy, and responsible for the precedent of a managed peacetime economy.

Unfortunately for Hoover's reputation, the essays are nearly unanimous in the appraisal that his programs were failures, including his "War on Waste," efforts at industrial democracy, and the early 1920s economic recovery measures. Varied and complex reasons are offered for the abundant failures amassed by Hoover. Some find the fault in inherently invalid assumptions upon which the associative state was based, which would have prevented its realization irrespective of the limitations of its principle architect. "the

---

[55]Hawley, Ellis W., ed., *Herbert Hoover as Secretary of Commerce: Studies in New Era Thought and Practice* (Iowa City: University of Iowa Press, 1981).

[56]Krog, Carl E. and William R. Tanner, eds., *Herbert Hoover and the Republican Era: A Reconsideration* (Lanham, MD: University Press of America, 1984).

Chief," however, is not allowed to escape criticism that easily. A preponderance of writers are also prone to emphasize Hoover's own contradictory, fuzzy, and inconsistent perceptions, flawed personality, and political ineptness as decisive for or contributing to his failures. The principled idealist with a humane and visionary outline of the associative state is often in graphic relief with the dogmatic and blundering practitioner.

Revitalization of ailing industries and impetus to new ones along associative state lines had been a popular topic since 1980, but one largely expounded in journals. Hoover's policies are pronounced as failures nearly without exception, but success is discerned in Philip T. Rosen, *The Modern Stentors: Radio Broadcasters and the Federal Government, 1920-1934*.[57] This well-written, extensively researched, and nicely synthesized book informs readers that Hoover was only one of the many principals in mercurial, early broadcast history, and that adoption of his particular views of private ownership, industry practices, and government regulation were anything but inevitable. The fact that nearly all aspects of radio broadcasting had "the Chief's" imprint attests to his aggressive bureaucratic acumen and infinite tenacity.

Hoover's lower stock as secretary of commerce is a preview to that as president. Few of the complimentary earlier revisionist versions are left unchallenged, and the Hoover evinced since 1980 is often a markedly less likable and more hapless figure. Not since the apex of the progressive interpretation has some of the writing been as devastating. Journals have been particularly scathing forums, and articles abound with testimony on his personal, political, and ideological deficiencies. The writing, however, should not be construed as a simple reversion to the progressive interpretation. Whereas progressive historians often

---

[57]Rosen, Philip T., *The Modern Stentors: Radio Broadcasters and the Federal Government, 1920-1934* (Westport, CT: Greenwood Press, 1980).

employed greater portions of emotion and ideology than reason and evidence, writers since 1980 often make their case with convincing evidence and astute analysis.

Writing of the post-1980 variety is also likely to give Hoover credit for unprecedented anticyclical measures. An interesting phenomenon is that when differences narrow they also loom larger between the New Era and the New Deal. Hoover transcended or sacrificed important aspects of the associative state vision that he regarded as nearly inviolate in the 1920s to combat the depression and generate economic recovery, but he could not and would not adopt unrestrained New Deal intervention. The halting and gloomy reluctance with which Hoover adopted policies that skewed or openly violated his economic tenets only accentuates differences between the tentative "Chief" and uninhibited New Dealers. Not unexpected, however, is that much recent writing on the presidency attaches greater importance than once was given to Hoover's political and personal deficiencies. Strongly inferred in a portion of the writing is that Hoover's political ineptitude, defective personality, and, one could add, bad luck were of such a magnitude that not even expansive New Dealism could have saved the occupant of the White House.

Many of these propositions are presented in a restrained and not unsympathetic way by Martin L. Fausold, *The Presidency of Herbert Hoover*.[58] This astute survey has an instructive introduction that explains the various influences on Hoover's view and personality, and is particularly interesting on his transition from sectarian to secular Quakerism. Committed to reform, including a "new social system," Hoover's political passivity and ineptitude and inability to shape and inspire public opinion were apparent even before his administration was shaken by the stock market crash and ensuing depression. Hoover responded to the crisis in an unprecedented manner, although his actions were often

---

[58]Fausold, Martin L., *The Presidency of Herbert Hoover* (Lawrence: University Press of Kansas, 1985).

concealed or poorly explained, obscured by optimistic statements, and distorted by critics who were often more myopic than the subject of their denigration.

Although Hoover was a victim of base partisanship, personal vindictiveness, and public misunderstanding, he often did little to help his situation and often made it worse by always looking at the "dark side first." Hoover was the unfortunate captive of his own personality and political principles, and he was probably even more dogmatic in clinging to dubious beliefs like non-partisanship than to his economic views. Although never an advocate of unconditional government intervention, Hoover's economic policies moved a great distance between 1929 and 1932. Yet Hoover's too little, too late departures did not prevent the economy from sinking to its nadir.

Hoover's liabilities had fewer international than domestic repercussions, and Fausold is generous in his foreign-policy appraisal. Recognizing Hoover as the pivotal policymaker in his administration, the author assigns high marks for his restraint and sound judgment in pursuing American interests in a way that was compatible with a large part of the globe. Notwithstanding compliments on foreign policy and credit for domestic reform and economic recovery efforts, Fausold concludes that the negative assessment of Hoover is both valid and unlikely to change. A large part of the post-1980 writing parallels Fausold's analysis and concurs with his evaluation.

A substantial part of Fausold's book is retold by Barber in *From New Era to New Deal,* which is not less instructive simply because it is no longer seismic news that Hoover's anticyclical activism during the Great Depression violated his associative state postulates.[59] Hoover subscribed to the Keynesian axiom that aggregate volume of spending determines macroeconomic system behavior. Although Hoover is often criticized for dogmatic inflexibility, his views

---

[59]Barber, *From New Era to New Deal.*

were fluid and that axiom is one of the few constants that explain his economic policies.

"The Chief" received his due in Barber's book, which analyzes his fluid views and responses to the economic disaster. Often off the mark, along with many economists, Hoover nevertheless moved almost inevitably in retrospect to broaden government responsibility and intervention. Even persons generally conversant with Hoover's policies may discover edifying information, like his effort, too successful for his later reputation, to obscure his "dramatic departures." "The Chief's" failure was due not to economic illiteracy, as that phrase is commonly understood, but to his inhibitions about the role of government. Hoover's unprecedented but circumscribed use of government resulted in "striking discontinuities" and "arresting continuities" between the New Era and the New Deal.

Barber's estimate of Hoover is higher than that of many post-1980 writers, whose interest is largely in political and social aspects of his administration. Essays in Krog and Tanner, *Herbert Hoover and the Republican Era*, for example, often portray a politically maladroit and intractable president whose principles and dogmatism were stronger than sound judgement and compassion. A shift in emphasis is also discernible in later writing, and racial minorities have obtained parity with destitute Americans as principal victims of Hoover's policies.

This is the thesis of many articles and the well-written and thoroughly researched book on the conundrum of race by Donald J. Lisio, *Hoover, Blacks, and Lily-Whites: A Study of Southern Strategies*.[60] Anything but a Hooverphobe, Lisio nevertheless concludes that "the Chief's" policies toward blacks were disastrous. Hoover had enlightened racial attitudes for his generation, but few of his high

---

[60]Lisio, Donald J., *Hoover, Blacks, and Lily-Whites: A Study of Southern Strategies* (Chapel Hill: University of North Carolina Press, 1985).

principles and policies went more seriously awry than those on race. His plan to end black subjugation through tenancy and peonage fizzled, and his strategy to benefit blacks through patronage reform that would lead to a two-party South was dubiously conceived and ineptly executed.

Unwillingness to disclose the black gains envisaged in the strategy and egregious political bungling led to the widespread and mistaken belief that Hoover had a lily-white southern strategy and was hostile to black rights and aspirations. Lisio describes a steady and pathetic deterioration of relations between Hoover and blacks, and a widening gulf between principles and practices. Hoover's losses as a consequence were largely self-inflicted. Although "more an unwitting victim of racism and of his own peculiar failings as a political leader than he was an enemy of black people," Hoover's "venture into southern politics proved a sad encounter both for him and black Americans."

Amply compensating for past inattention to the third of Hoover's life after the White House are the two works: Gary Dean Best, *Herbert Hoover, the Post-Presidential Years, 1933-1964*, and Richard Norton Smith, *An Uncommon Man: The Triumph of Herbert Hoover*.[61] Parallels are stronger than dissimilarities between the authors, and they dispel any notions that Hoover faded into obscurity, abandoned politics, or drastically altered his mind on any important issue. Best posits that "the Chief's" later career alone was influential enough to make an imprint on history, and neither he nor Smith leave many grounds for dispute.

Hoover lived with slander, spite, and public opprobrium after 1933, and was a pariah even within his party, which

---

[61]Best, Gary Dean, *Herbert Hoover, the Post-Presidential Years, 1933-1964*, 2 vols. (Stanford: Hoover Institution Press, 1983); Richard Norton Smith, *An Uncommon Man: The Triumph of Herbert Hoover* (New York: Simon & Schuster, 1984).

twice denied him renomination. Not one to suffer rejection with equanimity, he often answered his tormentors in a petty and vindictive spirit. Will power, political adroitness, longevity that surpassed enemies, public forgetfulness, and conciliatory gestures, for example, by Harry S Truman enabled Hoover to regain respect, influence, and a sense of proportion.

Progressive by earlier standards, Hoover was conservative by later ones—if the last appellation is not distorted. Without renouncing welfare capitalism, he balked at intrusive government, and his foreign policy views were a blend of isolationism and internationalism. When Hoover's age and health curtailed his public activity, he became even more compulsive about writing. Prolific if not riveting, his writing was strongly didactic, reflected his particular vision, and expressed his personal version of the past. Hoover despaired about America, but he died at the age of ninety with his faith preserved.

Best has written excellent political biography that does not deviate long or far from the subject; Hoover's myriad interests and prodigious activities are left largely unexplored. Interesting and perceptive vignettes in the Smith biography are an instructive supplement to the Best narrative. Competing viewpoints are often omitted or summarily dismissed in the Best volumes, with the consequence that they can be read like a Hoover monologue. Best is convincing that "the Chief" would be an ideal fishing companion, except for the one-sided conversation. Although deferential toward his subject, Smith is less hesitant to impute frailty and error to Hoover.

The initial favorable revisionist portrayal of Hoover that gained many adherents has been qualified in the writing since 1980, but it does not amount to a categorical scuttling of earlier revisionism nor the reinstitution of the progressive interpretation. Writing in this decade, in fact, contains many affirmations of earlier revisionism, and many of the differences reflect a logical progression in historical interpretation. Whatever the criticisms and failures of Hoover, they are not of a nineteenth-century reactionary; they are of an early twentieth-century progressive whose philosophical bridge between the past and the future was buckled by the weight that it had to carry. Although historians have recently emphasized "the Chief's" political, personality, and doctrinal limitations, the initial revisionist view of an able and activist reform-minded secretary of commerce and president is dented but intact.

Martin L. Fausold concluded in his perceptive book on the Hoover presidency that the negative evaluation of "the Chief" was unlikely ever to change. Progressive historians, of course, subscribed to the same proposition. Prediction is perilous business, but it seems safe to suggest that Hoover may well be a subject of nearly infinite revision. This is both because many varieties of historians write in habitually changing contexts and because Hoover, as illustrated in the famous "Ding" Darling cartoon, was a man for all interpretations.

The historical interpretations of Hoover have now made nearly a full revolution, and the currently revised Hoover has many of the same characteristics that first made him attractive to his contemporaries. Although historians of this generation are conscious of Hoover's frailties and failures, they also have an appreciation of his decency, integrity, and humaneness that an earlier generation repressed. The revisionist reconstruction of "the Chief" has enabled him to receive the respect that evaded him in his own lifetime. The mills of historical revisionism can grind slowly but they finally ground fair in the instance of Hoover.

Herbert Hoover and Foreign Policy: A Retrospective Assessment

Alexander DeConde

> This is a slightly revised version of the essay appearing in *Herbert Hoover Reassessed: Essays Commemorating the Fiftieth Anniversary of the Inauguration of Our Thirty-First President*. Senate Document No. 96-63, 96th Congress, 2nd Session. Washington, DC: GPO, 1981.

Most biographers, historians, and others who have explored the presidency of Herbert C. Hoover (1929-1933) have focused on his domestic policies, especially on his struggle with the Great Depression. Usually they have expressed strong feelings either for or against him. Writers of liberal persuasion have generally depicted him as an emotionless reactionary who had taken on a job beyond his capabilities. Friendly biographers, often journalists, and other writers on the conservative side, have defended Hoover's policies and have pictured him as a kindly man, a great humanitarian, misunderstood by his people and deliberately maligned by opponents seeking political advantage.[1]

In recent years scholars who have examined previously closed Hoover archives have written a number of balanced and relatively unemotional assessments of the Hoover presidency. Several of them have concentrated on his record in foreign relations within a reasonably detached

---

[1] For a recent assessment of key literature on Hoover as president, see Donald R. McCoy, "Trends in Viewing Herbert Hoover, Franklin D. Roosevelt, Harry S. Truman and Dwight D. Eisenhower," *The Midwest Quarterly* 20 (Winter 1979), 117-136; and for Hoover's ideas in his own words, see Kathleen Tracey, comp., *Herbert Hoover—A Bibliography: His Writings and Addresses* (Stanford, CA: Hoover Institution Press, 1977).

perspective.² To date, however, no one has written a book-length account of Hoover's role in the shaping of foreign policy, even though in that area presidents have frequently exercised their greatest power, and even though much of importance in foreign affairs occurred during Hoover's presidency. Scholars concerned with foreign policy have devoted more attention to the attitudes and ideas of his secretary of state, Henry L. Stimson, than to Hoover's own views and predilections in international affairs. The one book that covers the foreign relations of the Hoover presidency as a whole concentrates on the "Hoover-Stimson foreign policy" and gives as much attention to the secretary of state as it does to the president.³

This apparent slighting of Hoover as the dominant figure in the foreign policy of his own administration is unusual in several respects. In few instances in the American past have secretaries of state captured, as shapers of policy, more attention than the presidents to whom they were always subordinate. Secondly, Hoover was neither a passive personality nor an acquiescent president, especially in the area of foreign relations. Historian Carl N. Degler even maintains that "he was unquestionably one of the truly activist presidents of our history." Having "great confidence in his own ability," as recent studies of greater depth also point out, Hoover wanted to be, and usually was, in direct command of foreign policy.⁴ He did not even permit special advisers to

---

²See particularly the philosophically divergent essays by Selig Adler, "Hoover's Foreign Policy and the New Left," and Joan Hoff Wilson, "A Reevaluation of Herbert Hoover's Foreign Policy," in M.L. Fausold and G.T. Mazuzan, eds. *The Hoover Presidency* (Albany: State University of New York Press, 1974), 153-186.

³Robert H. Ferrell, *American Diplomacy in the Great Depression: Hoover-Stimson Foreign Policy, 1929-1933* (New Haven, CT: Yale University Press, 1957).

⁴The first quotation comes from Carl N. Degler, "The Ordeal of Herbert Hoover," *The Yale Review* 52 (Summer 1963), 571; and the second from Melvyn P. Leffler, *The Elusive Quest: America's Pursuit of European Stability and French Security, 1919-1933* (Chapel Hill: University of North Carolina Press, 1979), 229. Leffler suggests, on the basis of persuasive evidence, that Hoover's

share his power in this area. No Edward M. House, Henry Kissinger, or Zbigniew Brzezinski had a hand in the shaping of foreign policy within the Hoover administration. Thirdly, by experience, intellectual capacity, and disposition Hoover seemed much better qualified to handle the nation's foreign relations than were his two immediate predecessors in the White House, or even most of his high ranking contemporaries in politics.

More than any previous presidents, with the possible exception of John Quincy Adams, Hoover knew from firsthand experience before entering the White House something about foreign peoples. For years, as a mining engineer, he had traveled widely abroad, living in Australia, China, other parts of Asia, Russia, Africa, and in Europe. During the First World War, beginning in 1914, he entered public life by working in Belgium and elsewhere in Europe administering relief to war-ravaged peoples. In the process he cooperated with or clashed with Belgian, Dutch, British, French, and German officials, military and civilian. When he returned to the United States he served as President Woodrow Wilson's Food Administrator. He also became one of Wilson's trusted advisers, gaining appointment to the American War Council in March 1918. There Hoover became involved in major presidential decisions and at times influenced them.

Hoover's thinking on international politics at this time appears to have pivoted on a changing and perhaps too personal a perception of Europeans. Before the war in the course of living in Europe, he had acquired an appreciation for its art, literature, architecture, and grand style of life. The war, he believed, had transformed the gracious Europe he had known in his early years into a "furnace of hate." During the period of the armistice and at the peace conference, where he served on twenty committees and as chairman of six, he

ideas were the dominant ones in Republican policy throughout the twenties. Norman A. Graebner, "Hoover, Roosevelt, and the Japanese," in Dorothy Borg and Shumpel Okamoto, eds., *Pearl Harbor as History: Japanese-American Relations, 1931-1941* (New York: Columbia University Press, 1973), 25-26, also stresses Hoover's importance as a maker of policy.

had to work closely with leaders of this transformed Europe. Once again he collided with them, this time mainly with British, French, and Italian officials. This bruising experience in international diplomacy, where he discerned "national intrigue, selfishness, nationalism, heartlessness, rivalry and suspicion," deepened his disillusionment with the affairs of the Old World.[5]

Whether or not his attitude stemmed from a realistic appraisal of world affairs, he came to distrust Europe and Europeans, believing that their leaders were somehow conspiring to keep the United States off balance through involvement in their seemingly endless political quarrels. In particular he nurtured a deep antipathy to Marxist Russia, going so far in March 1919 as to urge Wilson to manipulate or withhold food supplies desired by Russians so as "to stem the tide of Bolshevism." [6]

In September 1919 Hoover left Paris and returned to the United States with a glowing reputation as a humanitarian, as the war's foremost civilian hero, and as a major political figure. He also carried with him the conviction that the peacemakers at Paris had in the Treaty of Versailles created a document of vengeance, and that for this and other reasons the United States should avoid further entanglement in Europe's politics. In accordance with this view he advised the president to keep the United States out of the various international economic and military commissions spawned by

---

[5]The quotation comes from Joseph S. Davis, "Herbert Hoover, 1874-1964: Another Appraisal," *The South Atlantic Quarterly* 47 (Summer 1969), 300.

[6]See the commentary of Murray N. Rothbard in Ellis W. Hawley et al., *Herbert Hoover and the Crisis of American Capitalism* (Cambridge, MA: Schenkman, 1973), 124-125; David Burner, *Herbert Hoover: A Public Life* (New York: Knopf, 1978), 120; and Richard Hofstadter, "Herbert Hoover and the Crisis of American Individualism," in his *The American Political Tradition and the Men Who Made It* (New York: Knopf, 1948), 292-293, for examples of Hoover's anti-Soviet attitude.

the treaty. Yet he also believed that European economic rehabilitation depended on the treaty and that the United States, because of its alleged moral superiority and its greater economic and political power, should assume a role of detached but not indifferent leadership in world affairs. He favored economic coordination, if not close cooperation, between great powers to form a worldwide economic community led by the United States.

Despite his distrust of Europe, Hoover publicly espoused some form of collective security, or cooperation with other nations in working for peace. In 1920, for instance, he campaigned for the League of Nations, but attempted to distinguish between the Treaty of Versailles and the League. Even though he disliked the treaty, he urged its approval, essentially because the League covenant was an integral part of the treaty and Americans could not have one without the other. Like Wilson, he at first opposed reservations attached by the Senate to its proposed approval of the treaty, but later he urged the president to accept them. Even the "undesirable" reservations, Hoover told Wilson on November 19, 1919, "do not seem to imperil the great principle of the League of Nations to prevent war." [7]

Still later, after defeat of the League in the Senate, Hoover as secretary of commerce in the cabinets of Warren G. Harding and Calvin Coolidge had a voice in all important matters involving international economic policy and an active interest in other areas of foreign relations. In Hoover's hands the relatively new and small department of commerce acquired considerable power with influence ranging throughout government, leading a colleague in the treasury department to quip that he was "Secretary of Commerce and

---

[7]Quoted in Gary Dean Best, *The Politics of American Individualism: Herbert Hoover in Transition, 1918-1921* (Westport, CT: Greenwood Press, 1975), 32.

Under-Secretary of all other departments."[8] Hoover used the department of commerce as an instrument for promoting American financial interests abroad, mainly by uncovering unexploited opportunities for investments and fresh markets for surplus products.

Hoover also had a part in the Harding administration's most important venture in foreign policy, a nine-power naval arms conference. When the delegates convened in Washington in November 1921 Secretary of State Charles Evans Hughes sought Hoover's advice, particularly on matters pertaining to Asia. In the sensitive area of race and ethnicity, Hoover did not rise above the dominant prejudices of his time. He expressed disdain, if not contempt, for Japanese and other Asians, implying that they belonged to the "lower races." Later he deplored allegedly hyphenated allegiance among the "foreign-born" seeing in divided loyalties a menace to the kind of white, Protestant, patriotic Americanism he favored. In 1924, when Congress was setting racially and ethnically discriminatory immigration quotas, he favored exclusion of the Japanese, asserting that there were "biological and cultural grounds why there should be no mixture of Oriental and Caucasian blood."[9] He also regretted that "Nordics of all kinds" were being excluded from the United States while Puerto Ricans, essentially "undersized Latins," were being admitted.[10]

---

[8]Parker Gilbert quoted in Joseph Brandes, *Herbert Hoover and Economic Diplomacy: Department of Commerce Policy, 1921-1928* (Pittsburgh, PA: University of Pittsburgh Press, 1962), 39. See also Ellis W. Hawley, "Herbert Hoover, the Commerce Secretariat, and the Vision of an 'Associative State,' 1921-1928," *The Journal of American History* 41 (June 1974), 116-140, which explains Hoover's belief in a "superior American System."

[9]Quoted in Burner, *Hoover*, 197.

[10]Quoted in Theodore Friend, *Between Two Empires: The Ordeal of the Philippines, 1929-1946* (New Haven, CT: Yale University Press, 1965), 105. Joan Hoff Wilson, *Herbert Hoover: Forgotten Progressive*. (Boston: Little, Brown, 1975), 136, suggests that in

The literature on Hoover does not reveal how or to what extent his racial or ethnic attitudes influenced his views on foreign relations. Yet there must have been some overlap, for all during the 1920's he dealt with foreign issues and foreign peoples. Some of them at the time, such as the Japanese, more than likely discerned his scorn.

From 1922 to 1927 Hoover also served as an influential member of the World War Foreign Debt Commission. There he not only became deeply involved in one of the most perplexing problems in his country's relations with Europe but also had to deal with essentially the kind of European politicians for whom he had previously expressed distrust. Nonetheless, Hoover apparently liked the milieu of international politics because for a time he made obvious a desire to become Calvin Coolidge's secretary of state.

When Hoover ran for president in 1928, therefore, he had a considerable interest in foreign relations and broad experience in government, especially in matters involving foreign peoples and officials. In his thinking on international economics and politics he embodied the conventional wisdom of his time, with its faults as well as its virtues. He also brought to the campaign a reputation as an administrator of distinction, as a political and social progressive, and as an internationalist.[11] In keeping at least with the outward

---

dealing with blacks, Hoover did not show prejudice, whereas Gerald D. Nash in Hawley et al., *Herbert Hoover and the Crisis of American Capitalism*, 107, points out instances of racial bias and that black Americans considered him "the man in the lily White House."

[11]Scholars vary in their estimate of his progesive principles, and to what extent they influenced his views of foreign policy. Wilson, in *Hoover: Forgotten Progressive* stressed his progressivism; Elliot A. Rosen, *Hoover, Roosevelt, and the Brains Trust: From Depression to New Deal* (New York: Columbia University Press, 1977), 40, states flatly that "Hoover was no progressive;" Albert U. Romasco, *The Poverty of Abundance: Hoover, the Nation, the Depression* (New York: Oxford University Press, 1965), 16, argues that Hoover's philosophy "encompassed," in seeming contradiction, conservatism, progressivism, and liberalism; Ellis W Hawley in Hawley et al.,

aspects of internationalism, he expressed a willingness during the electioneering to work with the League, if he became president, in its non-political endeavors. In his inaugural address he accepted "the profound truth that our own progress, prosperity and peace are interlocked with ... [those] of all humanity." As a matter of political practicality, he also explained that Americans wanted "no political engagements such as membership in the League of Nations" because it might lead to foreign wars, and that he would respect their desire.[12]

Despite this record, various historians have assessed Hoover's performance in foreign policy as flawed because of his inexperience in rough-and-tumble domestic politics. They said, for example, that he simply "was not well equipped as a political animal" and that "his role as a politician does much to explain his failure in the White House.[13] While it is true that

Herbert Hoover and the Crisis of American Capitalism, 27, says Hoover was a "type of Progressive;" Craig Lloyd, *Aggressive Introvert: Herbert Hoover and Public Relations Management* (Columbus: Ohio State University Press, 1972), 102, emphasizes progressivism; Gary Dean Best, *The Politics of American Individualism: Herbert Hoover in Transition, 1918-1921* (Westport, CT: Greenwood, 1975), 178, insists that "Hoover was neither a progressive, nor an internationalist...but an American Individualist;" and David Burner and Thomas R. West, "A Technocrats Morality: Conservatism and Hoover the Engineer," in Stanley Elkins and Eric McKitrick, eds., *The Hofstadter Aegis: A Memorial* (New York: Knopf, 1974), 236, 251, 255-256, say that Hoover cannot easily be labeled and that he shifted from progressivism to conservatism.

[12]Washington, March 4, 1929, in William Starr Myers, *The State Papers and Other Public Writings of Herbert Hoover*, 2 vols.(New York: Doubleday, Doran, 1934), Vol. 1: 8-9. See also the favorable analysis in Edgar E. Robinson and Vaughn D. Bornet, *Herbert Hoover: President of the United States* (Stanford, CA: Hoover Institution Press, 1975), 97-99.

[13]The quotations come from Christopher Thorne, *The Limits of Foreign Policy: The West, the League and the Far Eastern Crisis of 1931-1933* (London: Putnam, 1972), 79, and Gerald D. Nash in Hawley et al., *Herbert Hoover and the Crisis of American Capitalism*, 88.

Hoover had not previously been elected to public office, several other presidents, among them George Washington and Dwight D. Eisenhower, had not had experience in national politics nor had they held noteworthy elective offices before becoming chief executive. Yet many writers praised rather than condemned them for their essentially non-political backgrounds.

In Hoover's case, the idea of political ineptness apparently began within his own party, and in issues related to foreign policy. Many old guard Republicans refused to forgive him for not having risen to prominence through the party ranks; they considered him something of a maverick. They also disliked his publicized internationalist outlook, his many years of residence in foreign countries, his early but flagging desire to bring the United States into the World Court, and his previous support of the League of Nations. In turn, their unbending isolationism annoyed him.[14] Yet, in part because of his nationalism grounded in the conviction of American superiority over other peoples, historians have often portrayed Hoover as an isolationist.[15] Even some of those who have viewed his conduct of foreign policy favorably have resorted to euphemisms such as "independent nationalism" to distinguish his policy from isolation and from

---

[14] See Jordan A. Schwarz, *The Interregnum of Despair: Hoover, Congress, and the Depression* (Urbana: University of Illinois Press, 1970), 47-50, and Harris G. Warren, *Herbert Hoover and the Great Depression* (New York: Oxford University Press, 1959), 25, 123, 152, 248, 301, which stresses old guard resentment.

[15] See, for example, Selig Adler, *The Isolationist Impulse: Its Twentieth Century Reaction* (New York: Abelard-Schuman, 1966), 208, 398, 400; Manfred Jones, "Isolationism," in Alexander DeConde, ed., *Encyclopedia of American Foreign Policy: Studies of the Principal Movements and Ideas*, 3 vols. (New York: Scribner, 1978), Vol. 2: 502; and John D. Hicks, *Republican Ascendancy, 1921-1933* (New York: Harper, 1960), 259. Liberal internationalists frequently interpreted Hoover's Presidency "as an era of darkness before the dawning of the New Deal," Adler, "Hoover's Foreign Policy and the New Left," 154.

an internationalism committed to an institutionalized collective security.[16]

Some scholars have tried to explain Hoover's foreign policy, as they have the whole of his presidency, in terms of his personality, his Quaker faith, his big business background, his old-fashioned nationalism, his devotion to capitalism, and his belief in individualism, or the idea that people, and nations too, should fight their own battles. Critics, and even those who claimed friendship, found him overly sensitive to criticism, humorless, insecure, inflexible, unforgiving, doctrinaire, and self-righteous. Somehow, they implied, these personal qualities affected his performance in foreign relations. They pointed out that his commitment to internationalism, rooted in the idea that the United States could help others by serving as a model, or essentially as the unique and superior nation destined to lead the benighted, was so restricted as to be void of real meaning.

Other critics, particularly liberal writers and academics of the thirties and forties who looked closely at Hoover's record and his words, found what they consider a similar weakness in his approach to his most cherished goal in international affairs—peace. As president, he aspired to a form of international cooperation devoid of coercion, a voluntary system that would on its own bring lasting peace to the world. Many statesmen, even cynical ones, have expressed faith in analogous ideals, but Hoover believed in his ideal with a consistency approaching religious commitment.[17] "It seems to me," he wrote in an analysis of foreign policy six months after taking office, "that there is the most profound

---

[16]See Wilson, "A Reevaluation of Hoover's Foreign Policy," 165, and Wilson, *Hoover: Forgotten Progressive*, 168.

[17]Richard N. Current is one of the first scholars to stress this. See his "The United States and 'Collective Security': Notes on the History of an Idea," in Alexander DeConde, ed., *Isolation and Security: Ideas and Interests in Twentieth-Century American Foreign Policy* (Durham, NC: Duke University Press, 1957), 5-51.

outlook for peace today that we have had at any time in the last half century."[18] Few, if any, writers have doubted his intense dislike for war, an attitude that seemed to grow logically out of his Quaker upbringing. Although so strongly pacifistic in his thinking that Stimson and others called him "a pacifist President," he was not a true pacifist. He did not rule out the use of force if deemed necessary, especially in defense of the continental United States.

This tilt toward pacifism influenced but did not necessarily shape important aspects of Hoover's foreign policy. He refused to take measures that risked a commitment to military action on behalf of abstract ideals, even those he found attractive, such as the concept of collective security. In keeping with his Quaker ideals, as president he stressed spiritual values, or the primacy of national moral force over the use of military violence, in foreign crisis. Moral persuasion, not armies, he felt, would bring to Americans and to all peoples the international as well as domestic security they sought.

Hoover expressed this aspect of his philosophy in foreign relations clearly in a speech on Armistice Day, November 11, 1929. He said that "the European nations have, by the covenant of the League of Nations, agreed that if nations failed to settle their differences peaceably then force should be applied by other nations to compel them to be reasonable. We have refused to travel this road. We are confident that at least in the Western hemisphere public opinion will suffice to check violence. This is the road we prepare to travel."

A few months later the president returned to this theme. The "vast majority" of Americans, he insisted, were opposed to "commitments to use force to maintain peace.... I believe it is clear that the United States can more effectively and wisely

[18]To Secretary of State, Washington, Sept. 17, 1929, *Papers Relating to the Foreign Relations of the United States, 1929*, 3 vols. (Washington, DC: GPO, 1943) Vol. 1: 24.

work for peace without commitments to use coercion to enforce settlements."[19]

Essentially, Hoover believed that collective persuasion, coupled with the power of moral force, rather than collective violence, no matter how righteous, would preserve peace. Such massive persuasion would, in his view, make the Kellogg-Briand Peace Pact, whereby signatories renounced war as an instrument of policy, effective. He did not reject the concept of collective security that he had previously embraced, but rather the military force deemed necessary by liberal theorists to make it work. He found reprehensible the idea that in the world community of nations majority will would keep non-conforming members in line through fear of unrelenting punishment. In explaining his thinking on this subject he frequently drew analogies between municipal and international law, claiming with exaggeration that consent rather than force served as the basis for both. These ideas, or similar ones, like themes in a symphony, occur again and again in his speeches and writings. Taken as a whole they represent a commitment to freedom of action within a philosophy of non-belligerent nationalism.

Yet, as some historians have pointed out, Hoover's ideas, actions, and reputation in foreign policy bristle with contradictions. In advocating free trade, support for the League of Nations, and entrance into the World Court he talked and behaved as an internationalist. In his insistence on high tariffs, in his distrust of Europe, in his ethnocentricity and in his support of immigration restriction he functioned not only as a nationalist but also as an isolationist. Regardless, he probably acted with no greater inconsistency in foreign relations than did most presidents.

Despite this mosaic of inconsistencies, a number of scholars view Hoover's thinking on war, peace, and world

---

[19]The quotations come from Armin Rappaport, *Henry L. Stimson and Japan, 1931-1933* (Chicago: University of Chicago Press, 1963), 35-36.

politics as important. They do so properly because his ideas, more than those of any other individual, shaped the foreign policy of his administration. He took pains to demonstrate that as president he not only carried on his person the responsibilities for foreign policy but also that in its main development it reflected his principles. Nonetheless, historians and political scientists generally do not consider him, in the jargon of academia, a "strong president" or an "imperial executive." He adhered to a strict constitutional interpretation of his office, mindful always, it seems, of the limitations rather than the grandeur of his presidential powers. Nowhere in his writings, or even in that of critics, can one find evidence that he deliberately sought to stretch his power in foreign relations beyond any previous limits in the name of national security, international stability, peace, or any other ambiguous ideal.

Even the Great Depression, signalled by the stock market crash of October 1929, within eight months after he had taken office, did not elicit from Hoover demands for greater power. According to the most prominent interpretation of this aspect of his presidency, the depression rather than the thrust of Hoover's ideas dominated the foreign policy of his administration. This assessment holds that the economic crisis prevented the president's policy, or principles, from becoming an effective force for peace; the depression produced a "timidity of statesmanship" rather than bold action. It crippled the world's diplomacy, presented aggressors a golden opportunity to strike, and "palsied the hands of American statesmen."[20] This analysis depicts Hoover as overwhelmed by events beyond his control. Circumstances rather than incompetence trapped him, and also his administration's foreign policy, in helplessness.

Whether or not he was diplomatically impotent within a web of economic paralysis, Hoover considered the depression a product of international affairs. He maintained

[20]Ferrell, *American Diplomacy in the Great Depression*, 5, 278.

that foreign economic problems, not just domestic ones, had caused the crippling crisis. Since in this theory the causes were global, only international financial measures could tame the depression and bring back prosperity to Americans.[21] "This depression," he said in October 1930, "is worldwide. Its causes and effects lie only partly in the United States." In June 1931 he explained the widespread financial crisis as part of "malign inheritances in Europe of the Great War.... Without the war, we should have no such depression."[22] In January 1932 he expressed a variation of this theme in ethnic terms. Only "the cooperation of the Anglo-Saxons," he said, could now rescue civilisation from disasters such as the depression; other peoples "could not be counted on."[23]

Hoover also used the depression to buttress his philosophy on tariffs. To protect itself against external economic disturbances, such as those that brought on the depression, he insisted, the United States had to maintain high tariff walls. Yet at the same time he wished to expand the sale of American products abroad; and to have free access to foreign raw materials, particularly those the United States did not possess. Such contradictions in his thinking, when viewed within the context of short-range national interests, may have at the time seemed pragmatic rather than muddled.

To Europeans, Latin Americans, and others, these ideas appeared not only confusing, but wrong. Hoover's public insistence that former partners in a common war effort must

---

[21]Scholars dispute this analysis. See, for example, Rosen, *Hoover, Roosevelt, and the Brains Trust*, 41, 53, who views Hoover's contention as "literally myopic." For a discussion of the relationship between European stability, world recovery, American well-being and Hoover, see Melvyn P. Leffler, "Political Isolationism, Economic Expansionism, or Diplomatic Realism: American Policy Toward Western Europe, 1921-1933," *Perspectives in American History* 8 (1974), 423.

[22]The quotations come from Romasco, *Poverty of Abundance*, 182, 185.

[23]Quoted in Thorne, *Limits of Foreign Policy*, 56.

pay their war debts made him unpopular in much of Europe. European leaders viewed the depression as conceived and born in America, in part because Americans insisted on debt repayment while maintaining high tariffs. Hoover had not always desired repayment. In 1922, as a member of the World War Foreign Debt Commission, he had initially favored writing off the war debts as a means of strengthening the "moral" posture of the United States. He retreated from this position when colleagues pointed out that Congress would not approve of anything that smacked of cancellation, but privately retained a willingness to consider some form of reduction if not outright cancellation. However, when Secretary of State Stimson wanted to cancel "these damn debts," the depression had stiffened Hoover's opposition to cancellation. This turned out to be one of the few of his policy decisions that apparently had wide popular support.

Hoover's action on the tariff, however, did not please large, vocal segments of American society. In June 1930, despite intense opposition from economists, businessmen, and internationalists who argued that it would gravely injure American foreign policy, he approved the Smoot-Hawley Tariff Act. Hoover felt that its high rates would aid farmers and protect the American standard of living without creating serious repercussions abroad. He argued in 1933 that "the American tariff did not strangle the buying power of foreign nations."[24] On this point he may have been correct, but on most counts historians as well as economists have condemned his defense of the tariff as wrongheaded. Harris G. Warren, an historian friendly to the Hoover presidency, concludes that "probably nothing was so damaging to Hoover's reputation during his first two years in the

---

[24]Wilson, "A Reevaluation of Hoover's Foreign Policy," 174. See also her *American Business and Foreign Policy, 1920-1933* (Lexington: University of Kentucky Press, 1971), 98.

presidency as his handling of the tariff." Warren considers the Hawley-Smoot Tariff a "political disaster."[25]

In another area of foreign economic relations, that of loans and investments abroad, Hoover shared the convictions of numerous contemporaries. He opposed further government loans to foreign countries, favoring instead private investments. He felt that private ventures would be less vulnerable to political pressures than would government commitments and would less likely lead to undesirable foreign entanglements. Yet the volume of private American money invested abroad worried him. Even though earlier he had considered German reparations and war debts as being "interlocked," as president he refused to admit, at least openly, any connection between them.[26] Nonetheless, these financial matters produced a crisis he could not ignore. It began in the spring of 1931 when Germany and Austria appeared on the verge of defaulting on private debts owed to American bankers. Such defaults would end German reparations payments to Allied governments which in turn would stop installments on their debts to the United States. Moreover, the defaults could trigger bank failures in the United States. After some hesitation the president took dramatic action on June 20, 1931, he proposed a moratorium of one year on the payments of war debts that European governments owed the United States if, in turn, they would similarly defer payments of war debts and reparations owed to them.

While still insisting publicly that debts and reparations were not linked, Hoover practically admitted with his moratorium scheme that debt payments in fact came out of German reparations. Regardless of such a connection, the moratorium, which all the concerned parties accepted, did not resolve the problem; it merely postponed collapse of the complicated system involving debts and reparations. Even

---

[25]Warren, *Hoover and the Great Depression*, 92.

[26]See Leffler, *Elusive Quest*, 55, 180-81, 200-07, and Wilson, "A Reevaluation of Hoover's Foreign Policy," 178-179.

though the Allies scaled-down the reparations, Germany eventually defaulted on its payment, and also on payment of private debts. Then America's debtors defaulted on their obligations. Nonetheless, in the views of some analysts, Hoover had in the case of the moratorium acted with promptness and "intelligent perception."[27]

In these various foreign policy matters Hoover supposedly "never pandered to popular sentiment." With disarmament, however, he demonstrated considerable anxiety over the state of public opinion, more than "on other controversial foreign policy issues."[28] This concern appears logical because he had a deep faith in disarmament, especially in the reduction of costly naval armaments. In his view, "the world should have relief from the sore burden of armaments." Moreover, he envisioned the reduction of budgets for weapons as about the only effective means of curbing militarism.[29]

Early in his administration Hoover took steps to convert these ideas, that linked peace with the control of armaments into working policy. In particular he attempted to strengthen the Briand-Kellogg Pact by utilizing it as a tool for constructing agreements on arms limitation, but with safeguards against possible American entanglement in the politics of the League or of other collective security

---

[27]Ethan Ellis, *Republican Foreign Policy, 1921-1933* (New Brunswick, NJ: Rutgers University Press, 1968), 26. For details, see Edward W. Bennett, *Germany and the Diplomacy of the Financial Crisis, 1931* (Cambridge, MA: Harvard University Press, 1962), 113-182.

[28]The quotations come from Wilson, *Business and Foreign Policy*, 59.

[29]New York, Feb. 13, 1933, quoted in William S. Myers and Walter H. Newton, *The Hoover Administration: A Documented Narrative* (New York: Scribner's, 1936), 301. Gerald E. Wheeler, *Prelude to Pearl Harbor: The United States Navy and the Far East, 1921-1931* (Columbia: University of Missouri Press, 1963), 156-7, briefly discusses the salient features of Hoover's concern for disarmament.

arrangements. In his thinking the anti-war pact formed the foundation for disarmament.[30]

When J. Ramsay MacDonald, prime minister in Great Britain's new Labour government, visited the United States in October 1929 and the two leaders conferred in the relaxed atmosphere of a presidential fishing camp on the banks of the Rapidan River in Virginia, they agreed sufficiently well, at least on matters of disarmament, for the British government to issue invitations to Japan, France, and Italy to join Britain and the United States in a previously planned five-power conference on naval problems. Although negotiations revealed fundamental differences among the powers, the London Naval Treaty they concluded in April 1930 called for a reduction in all categories of naval armaments. Never before had modern naval powers agreed to such limitation, which at the time seemed impressively sweeping. Hoover apparently looked upon the treaty as a personal victory and hoped it would stimulate further reductions in weapons and in time become a key element in a stable peace based on defensive armaments.

Those who favored large armaments, especially a big navy, seeing in them and not in words, instruments of true security, disliked the agreement. The Navy League, an organization devoted to lobbying for naval expenditures, quickly mounted a campaign for building the fleet to the limits of the London treaty. True to his anti-militarist convictions, the president opposed the program. On September 31, 1931, a congressional spokesman summarized the president's attitude. "Why should we build our navy up to the London Treaty limits," the congressman said apparently half seriously and half in jest, "when it will have nothing to do after we have built it.... No wars are on now and no war is in sight." Three weeks later Hoover announced a cut in naval construction for 1931-32 and elimination of all building for the following year. While he defended these measures as contributing to a stronger economy and to the cause of peace,

[30] See Raymond G. O'Connor, *Perilous Equilibrium: The United States and the London Naval Conference of 1930* (Lawrence: University of Kansas Press, 1962), 99, 49.

military men and others denounced the budget reductions. The Navy League accused Hoover of trying "at every turn to restrict, to reduce, to starve the Navy."[31]

Within his own intellectual limitations Hoover did act to reduce weapons of war and to create the kind of international peace system that fitted his ideas. In this context the London Naval Treaty was his most important accomplishment,[32] though he thought the limitation of armaments could move ahead through agreements for abolishing offensive weapons and retaining defensive arms. He proposed this idea to the World Disarmament Conference meeting in Geneva in June 1932, but it went nowhere even though he offered to reverse U.S. policy and accept "the right of [international arms] inspection" to verify compliance of treaties. Another proposal for a thirty per cent reduction in land as well as naval armaments met a similar fate there. Stimson compared this latter plan to an *Alice in Wonderland* fantasy.[33] Hoover's suggested arms reductions made no headway with foreign governments or with his own military experts. Historians, too, scoffed at his approach to disarmament, considering it barren of lasting achievement and hence a poor substitute for a solid commitment to collective security.

In a like manner Hoover also encountered difficulties in advancing his theories on the guarding of peace through collective moral persuasion. These ideas received their first practical test in a minor way in Asia. The experience began in the summer of 1929 when Nationalist China and the Soviet Union came to blows over control of a railroad in Manchuria.

---

[31]The Congressman quoted is Will R. Wood, chairman of the House Appropriations Committee, in Armin Rappaport, *The Navy League of the United States* (Detroit, MI: Wayne State University Press, 1962), 142, 144.

[32]O'Connor, *Perilous Equilibrium*, 117, emphasizes that the London treaty was Hoover's victory.

[33]See Ferrell. *American Diplomacy in the Great Depression*, 206-214; Leffler, *Elusive Quest*, 278-79; Burner, *Hoover*, 293; and Richard Dean Burns, "Origins of the United States' Inspection Policies, 1926-46," *Disarmament and Arms Control* [London] 2 (1964), 157-169.

Both countries had signed the Kellogg-Briand Pact and both had, thereby, committed themselves beforehand to settle disputes through peaceful means. The quarrel over Manchuria threatened no vital American interest, but as a sponsor of the anti-war treaty the United States, or at least its leaders, felt obligated to intervene politically. So Secretary of State Stimson asked the Chinese and Russians to honor their pledges, and even proposed a commission of conciliation to resolve the conflict. The belligerents and other governments refused to go along and the effort to invoke the Kellogg Pact antagonized the Soviets. They felt that the Hoover administration was siding with China, in part, because like his immediate predecessors, he refused to grant diplomatic recognition to the Soviet Union, although he tolerated unofficial trade relations.[34]

The failure to salvage peace in Manchuria through the diplomacy of moral commitment led Hoover to favor strengthening the Kellogg Pact with a third article specifying conciliation so that the machinery for settlement would be on hand when needed. He never transformed this idea into reality.[35] The tiff with the Soviets also demonstrated to Stimson, but not to Hoover, the futility of relying essentially on moral persuasion to keep the peace.

Stimson's attitude toward collective diplomacy subsequent to this small-scale crisis, as well as a fundamental difference in temperament, led to several clashes with the president. Both men were strong-willed and wished, or were determined, to run the show in foreign relations. Stimson believed in using the military establishment as an arm of diplomacy, and viewed as quite logical the employment of force as a matter of policy.

[34]See Themistocles C. Rodis, "Russo-American Contacts During the Hoover Administration," *South Atlantic Quarterly* 51 (April 1952), 235, 238, 244, and Joan Hoff Wilson, *Ideology and Economics: American Relations with the Soviet Union, 1918-1933* (Columbia: University of Missouri Press, 1974), 101-102.

[35]See Ferrell, *American Diplomacy in the Great Depression*, 82; and Harold Josephson, "Outlawing War: Internationalism and the Pact of Paris," *Diplomatic History* 3 (Fall 1979), 283.

Hoover, on the other hand, disliked soldiers, and particularly the application of military tactics to the conduct of foreign policy. "Instinctively," he wrote, "Mr. Stimson's first love was the law; and his second, the military field. Mentally, he was a mixture of a soldier and an advocate."[36] Some historians argue that Hoover exaggerated the personal difficulties with Stimson, and that although the differences between the two men may have made the conduct of foreign policy unnecessarily awkward, they did not weaken the effect of policy once it had been determined. Other scholars maintain that the philosophical conflict was basic and touched the essentials of Hoover's foreign policy. Whether the differences were truly minor or major made little difference in the relationship. What counted was Hoover's attitude. He perceived the differences as fundamental.[37]

The discord between the two men stands out most clearly in their attitudes toward the Manchurian crisis of 1931, the most dangerous and important international episode of the Hoover presidency. When Japan invaded Manchuria the fighting there, as in 1929, did not threaten American security, nor did it menace other tangible American interests. China sought help against the Japanese through existing instruments of collective action, essentially the League of Nations, the Nine Power Open Door Treaty of 1922, and the Kellogg-Briand Peace Pact of 1928. As a principal signatory of the

---

[36]*The Memoirs of Herbert Hoover*, 3 vols. (New York: Macmillan, 1951-52); Vol. 2: 219.

[37]For varying assessments of the relationship, see Ferrell, *American Diplomacy in the Great Depression*, 40; Elting E. Morison, *Turmoil and Tradition: A Study of the Life and Times of Henry L. Stimson* (Boston: Houghton-Mifflin, 1960), 404, 445-446; Thorne, *Limits of Foreign Policy*, 161, 199, 300, 416; Manfred Jones, "The United States and the Failure of Collective Security in the 1930's," in John Braeman, et al., eds., *Twentieth Century American Foreign Policy* (Columbus: Ohio State University Press, 1971), 263; Richard N. Current, "Henry Stimson, 1899-1933," in Norman A. Graebner, ed., *An Uncertain Tradition: American Secretaries of State in the Twentieth Century* (New York: McGraw-Hill, 1961), 172-173; Adler, "Hoover's Foreign Policy and the New Left," 156; and Graebner, "Hoover, Roosevelt, and the Japanese," 27.

latter two treaties the United States therefore became involved in the diplomacy of that distant war.

Although within the administration influential officials expressed sympathy for Japan, Hoover and Stimson as the crisis deepened came to regard her as the aggressor and a threat to world peace. Immersed in the domestic problems of the depression, the president at first did not pay much attention to the events in Asia. He permitted Stimson considerable leeway in responding to the crisis; indeed, the secretary of state even complained of difficulty in gaining access to the president. No responsible member of the government desired taking the lead in resolving the conflict between Japan and China. Hoover expressed this concern more emphatically in a cabinet meeting in October 1931, saying that he would not allow the League to deposit that "baby on America's doorstep."[38] He stood firm against any involvement, even indirectly, that might possibly pull the country into war.

As the violence in Manchuria intensified, the secretary of state came to desire what appeared as strong measures against Japan, more or less on the theory that collective action could or might deter her aggressiveness through fear of punishment. He could not, however, shake the president's opposition to such involvement, but he did manage to persuade Hoover that limited cooperation with League of Nations without commitment to action might contribute to peace. The president therefore permitted Stimson to assign an American diplomat, Prentiss B. Gilbert, as an observer at the meetings of the Council of the League of Nations as it took up the Manchurian question. Even this cautious step brought growls of disapproval from inflexible isolationists who insisted on no American involvement whatsoever. However timidly, Hoover and Stimson now went ahead and placed the United States on the side of those "new principles of international morality" decreeing that a threat of war concerned everyone, not just those doing the fighting.

---

[38]Thorne, *Limits of Foreign Policy*, 156, and Henry L. Stimson and McGeorge Bundy, *On Active Service in Peace and War* (New York: Harper, 1948), 232.

In support of this idea the two men worked out a doctrine of nonrecognition as a corollary to the Kellogg-Briand Pact. In a cabinet meeting in November 1931 Hoover recalled that Woodrow Wilson's secretary of state, William Jennings Bryan, had used nonrecognition in another Sino-Japanese confrontation in 1915. Stimson adopted Bryan's concept, and on January 7, 1932, enunciated a new version in identical notes to China and Japan. The United States would not, he said, recognize territorial changes produced by force that violated its treaty rights. Beyond this condemnation of Japanese expansion through publicized nonrecognition Hoover and Stimson could not agree.

Unknown to the public and to foreign statesmen at the time, Hoover conceived nonrecognition as a final step in a policy of collective persuasion, "the ultimate extension of the Kellogg-Briand Pact." Nonrecognition's only power would come from the moral judgment of people, or in other words, from the pressure of public opinion. He believed that the Nine-Power Treaty and the anti-war pact were "solely moral instruments based upon the hope that peace in the world can be held by the rectitude of nations and enforced solely by the moral reprobation of the world."[39]

Stimson, on the other hand, viewed nonrecognition as a preliminary measure within a process of coercive collective security. If necessary, he would backup nonrecognition with economic and military sanctions, imposed by the League of Nations and the United States, against the aggressor. If economic sanctions failed he would then be willing to join in collective military action to enforce the will of the majority nations. Hoover, who had come to think of Stimson as "more of a warrior than a diplomat." felt that sanctions would provoke the Japanese to war.[40] He considered Stimson's idea of fighting a war to enforce peace illogical.

---

[39]The first quotation comes from Josephson, "Outlawing War," 284, and the second from William S. Myers, *The Foreign Policies of Herbert Hoover*, 1929-1933 (New York: Scribner's, 1940), 156.

[40]Hoover, *Memoirs*, Vol. 2: 336.

Although willing to resort to war in defense of American soil, the president would not risk battle for a vague ideal in distant Asia. Moreover, he felt that in the long run the Chinese would absorb or expel the Japanese. In view of these differences between Hoover and Stimson some historians, notably Charles A. Beard and Richard N. Current, have insisted that the Hoover administration created two relatively distinct nonrecognition concepts—a Hoover and a Stimson doctrine. Other historians, such as Robert Ferrell and Roland Stromberg, deny the existence of two separate nonrecognition doctrines, and consider the differences between the president and the secretary of state on this issue as inconsequential.[41]

According to this latter analysis Stimson agreed basically with Hoover that sanctions would mean war. The secretary did not wish to precipitate violent conflict; he sought only to threaten the imposition of sanctions so as to bring Japan into line. Hoover, however, refused to use veiled menace and would not in any case stoop to anything that suggested dissimulation. He was convinced anyway that the Japanese would call any bluff he would attempt and that war would follow. As matter of record, he insisted that the United States would cooperate with the League in matters "of negotiation and conciliation." But, he said, "that is the limit. We will not go along on war or any of the sanctions either economic or military, for those are the roads to war."[42]

At Stimson's urging the League adopted the generalized principle of nonrecognition and condemned Japan as an aggressor. When a month later the Japanese announced they

---

[41] Charles A. Beard, *American Foreign Policy in the Making, 1932-1940* (New Haven, CT: Yale University Press, 1946), 134-136; Richard N. Current, "The Stimson Doctrine and the Hoover Doctrine," *American Historical Review* 59 (April 1954), 513-542; Current, *Secretary Stimson: A Study in Statecraft* (New Brunswick, NJ: Rutgers University Press 1954), 104-113; Ferrell, *American Diplomacy in the Great Depression*, 169n; Roland Stromberg, *Collective Security and American Foreign Policy: From the League of Nations to NATO* (New York: Praeger, 1963), 76-78; and Jonas, "Failure of Collective Security," 232, 257, 263.

[42] Hoover, *Memoirs*, Vol. 2, 370.

would withdraw from the League, the League did not impose sanctions and the American government did nothing on its own to implement such a policy. During the Hoover presidency, and after, the nonrecognition doctrine failed to keep peace or to force the Japanese out of Manchuria.[43] In later years most scholars who analyzed Asian policy termed nonrecognition a mistake.

Ironically, Hoover and Stimson quarreled over who should have credit for the doctrine.[44] The public, the press, and academicians usually associated it with Stimson, and invariably called it the Stimson Doctrine. Bedeviled by criticism of his domestic policies, Hoover felt that he needed a dramatic and important achievement in foreign policy to enhance his status among his people. Seemingly in desperation he clutched at the nonrecognition doctrine as such an accomplishment, touting it as the most important principle in foreign affairs advanced during his presidency. He convinced himself in 1932 that the nonrecognition notes "would take rank with the greatest papers of this country."[45]

In this instance Hoover's thinking appears obviously wishful. Whether or not justifiably, many historians, particularly those of liberal persuasion, assess not only nonrecognition as a failure but also dismiss Hoover's entire Asian policy as flawed. They insist that if he had taken a tough stance against Japan's carefully orchestrated violence in Manchuria as an unacceptable violation of the treaty structure

---

[43] William A. Williams, an historian noted for rehabilitating Hoover's reputation, underwent a change of attitude toward Hoover, acknowledged in his *The Contours of American History* (Cleveland: World, 1961), 426n. At one point, in "The Legend of Isolationism in the 1920's," *Science and Society* 18 (Winter 1954), 20, Williams argues that Hoover's attitude on nonrecognition "opened the door to appeasement." Later, in *The Tragedy of American Diplomacy* (rev. ed., New York: Dell, 1962), 164, he praises Hoover for refusing to court war.

[44] See Current, "Stimson," in Graebner, ed., *Uncertain Tradition*, 172; and Burner, *Hoover*, 295n.

[45] Stimson diary, entry of January 26, 1932, quoted in Stimson and Bundy, *On Active Service*, 244.

of the nineteen twenties, the Second World War might have been, or could have been, avoided. They argue, in a manner congenial to Henry Stimson's ideas, that Hoover should have taken calculated risks to halt the Japanese.[46]

On the other hand, most historians who deal with Hoover's Latin American policy consider it an area of positive, though moderate, achievement. On a pre-inauguration tour of ten southern republics, he announced repeatedly his opposition to United States intervention in the affairs of Latin America. Instead of acting as a neighborhood policeman, brandishing a big stick, the United States should, he said, behave as a good neigbor interested in the welfare of sister republics. After becoming president he denounced dollar diplomacy, cautiously repudiated the Roosevelt corollary to the Monroe Doctrine, and practiced what he had preached earlier by avoiding forcible intervention in the Latin countries. He pulled Marines out of Nicaragua, thereby ending an occupation of twenty years. Although he did not withdraw the United States troops stationed in Haiti, he set in motion machinery that terminated the military occupation shortly after he left office. The Hawley-Smoot tariff, however, aroused widespread resentment throughout Latin America. Nonetheless, when Hoover left the White House he had reversed a number of policies that had in the past earned the United States ill-will throughout much of the Western Hemisphere. For the first time in decades Latin Americans indicated some friendliness toward the United States. Hoover had, according to conventional scholarship, formulated the essentials of a good neighbor policy that would ripen and bear fruit in the next administration.[47]

[46]For details see Adler, "Hoover's Foreign Policy and the New Left," 155-156.

[47]See Alexander DeConde, *Herbert Hoover's Latin American Policy* (Stanford: Hoover Institution Press, 1951); Ellis, *Republican Foreign Policy, 1921-1933*, 228; Williams, *Contours of American History*, 436; Robert Ferrell, "Repudiation of a Repudiation," *Journal of American History* 51 (March 1965), 669-73, which stresses Hoover's reluctance to support renunication of the Roosevelt corollary; Donald Dozer, *Are We Good Neighbors? Three Decades of InterAmerican Relations, 1930-1960* (Gainesville: University of Florida Press,

Hoover applied to Latin America many of the same ideas he employed in other areas of foreign policy, essentially a reliance on moral suasion and aversion to the use of force. Yet he also aggressively promoted the expansion of United States capitalism abroad and accepted the racist ideology implicit in prevailing ideas that whites were inherently superior to people of color. Paradoxically, he also professed belief in what seemed in his time an old fashioned anti-imperialism. This mixture of faith in white supremacy and dislike of imperialism motivated him when confronted with the question of independence for the Philippine Islands.

Agricultural and labor pressure groups, seeking to end competition from Philippine tobacco, sugar, and coconut oil, and for racial reasons desiring to cut off Filipino immigration into the United States, urged independence for the islands. Although professing solicitude for liberty and anti-colonialism, the majority in Congress easily accepted the reasoning of the pressure groups. In December 1932 Congress passed the Hare-Hawes-Cutting bill that granted the Philippines independences after a transition of ten years. During this period the United States would continue to supervise and protect the islands, but Filipinos would enjoy a limited autonomy called commonwealth, or a status of dependency modified by partial self-government.

Opposed to colonies as a matter of principle, Hoover maintained in his later writings that he favored independence for the Philippines, and believed that their separation from the United States should be "complete and absolute."[48] Americans should not retain naval bases there and henceforth should not assume responsibility for the fate of the islands.

1959), 9-16; Bryce Wood, *The Making of the Good Neighbor Policy* (New York: Columbia University Press, 1961), 123-135; and Earl R. Curry, *Hoover's Dominican Diplomacy and the Origins of the Good Neighbor Policy* (New York: Garland, 1979), which argues that Hoover did not lay the foundations of the good neighbor policy because he did not commit himself "to absolute nonintervention," 255.

[48]Hoover, *Memoirs*, Vol. 2, 359.

Stimson fought against independence, urging continued control through the commonwealth arrangement. Hoover realized that with this device the United States could camouflage its colonialism and retain a base of power in Asia, but he refused to resort to such tactics. "Well," he said, "that's the white man's burden." Hoover therefore vetoed the bill, thinking also apparently that Filipino leaders desired such action.[49] Congress overrode his veto, and later the Filipino legislature rejected semi-independence. Ultimately, feeling they could obtain no better terms, Filipinos accepted such status under the commonwealth plan.

Along with his antipathy to imperialism, Hoover shunned the philosophical trappings of the imperial executive who sought to enhance the personal power of the president while enlarging the American imperium under the justification of national security.[50] In the words of a recent assessment, he "recognized logical limits to which the power of the state could be used in domestic and foreign affairs."[51] Hoover looked upon forcible intervention in the affairs of small nations or in controversies of major powers, as an act of last resort, not as a routine instrument of power. As with most national leaders, some of his thinking on foreign policy suffers from ambiguity, but his views and actions concerning non-intervention, anti-imperialism, and avoidance of war, fall into a reasonably clear and consistent pattern. In December 1937 as a private citizen commenting on Japan's invasion of China he repeated his earlier views, "There are plenty of ways that we can establish our honor and our dignity without going to war over questions of this sort." We should resort

---

[49] The quotation comes from Current, *Secretary Stimson*, 120. Hoover later claimed in *Memoirs*, Vol. 2: 361, that Filipino leaders desired the veto, but Friends, *Between Two Empires*, 104, says they did not and that Hoover's "memory was often faulty." For more on this point see Gerald E. Wheeler, "Republican Philippine Policy, 1921-1933," *Pacific Historical Review* 8 (Nov. 1959), 383, 387-390.

[50] Leffler, "Political Isolationism, Economic Expansionism, or Diplomatic Realism," 461, points out that Hoover did not equate all goals of American foreign policy with national security.

[51] Wilson, "A Reevaluation of Hoover's Foreign Policy," 184.

to war only "as the answer to assaults upon our national freedom and this alone."[52]

This strain of consistency, and much else in Hoover's foreign policy, does not throw off a bright light because it reflects no large tangible, and easily visible accomplishment, such as would have been the case if he had led the nation to victory in a great war. Instead, it illuminates, perhaps poorly, most often what he refused to do. Within a four-year period he turned aside more opportunities to use American power in foreign interventions than did any of the presidents of the twentieth century over a similar span of time. Writers of liberal and internationalist predilection usually have expressed admiration for the active interventionists among these executives, but they have generally portrayed Hoover as a negative force in foreign policy. Hoover's successor, at least in this area, reacted more generously; he believed that "old Hoover's foreign policy has been pretty good."[53] Liberal scholars have usually praised "strong" presidents, who relished responsibility, courted international adventure, and expanded personal power.

In some of his thinking on foreign policy, Hoover may have been nearsighted, sometimes racist, and often isolationist, particularly in later years, but he did not lead the country into any belligerent, ideological foreign crusade, or into any violent intervention or "police action" against small countries. He maintained peace in the crisis of Manchuria when some of his closest advisers considered war with Japan a logical, even imminent, possibility. He did not allow power to corrupt him, nor did he use his power in foreign relations to offset his domestic troubles. He considered himself accountable to Congress, to the people, and however vaguely, to the opinion of humanity.

These qualities, and especially some of Hoover's later activities pertaining to foreign policy, appealed to revisionist

[52]Gary Dean Best, "Totalitarianism or Peace; Herbert Hoover and the Road to War, 1939-1941," *Annals of Iowa* 54 (Winter 1979), 516.

[53]Franklin D. Roosevelt quoted in Frank Freidel, *Franklin D. Roosevelt: Launching the New Deal* (Boston: Little, Brown, 1974), 103.

historians of the forties and fifties. Liberal scholars, however, pictured him in these years as an unbending isolationist and compulsive anti-communist. Later, after his death in 1964, particularly in the era of the Vietnam War, many of the values he exemplified as president and also his later thinking on foreign policy received plaudits from scholars of various persuasions, but especially from new left historians and disillusioned liberals. They saw much to acclaim in his aversion to the use of force as a tool of foreign policy. Those of the left and right hailed him as a prophet of globalism who had warned against the evils of limitless military ventures abroad According to historian William A. Williams, "he was consistently opposed to the assumptions and attitudes that produced the cold war." [54]

Be that as it may, Hoover's foreign policy, however, has to be judged not by its rhetoric, or by that of its friends, or by Hoover's ideas after he left the presidency, but by its conduct within the limits of the four years he held command. From the perspective of almost a half-century some aspects of that policy, such as support for high tariffs, an ethnocentric isolationism, and an assumption that white, Anglo-Saxons had the necessary superior qualities to lead the world, still seem flawed, or at least questionable in wisdom. On the other hand what happened to the United States in world affairs within that half-century has caused historians to place the fundamentals of Hoover's foreign policy—the unwillingness to risk war for vague ideas or dubious causes, restraint in the use of coercion in any form, and a commitment to peace so firm that during his presidency no Americans died in overseas ventures or organizing violence—in fresh perspective. Scholars of various persuasions, as a consequence, consider Hoover's foreign policy as a whole worthy of reconsideration. Few now disparage it as negative, and within its limitations quite a few deem it praiseworthy.

---

[54]William A. Williams, *Some Presidents from Wilson to Nixon* (New York: Vintage, 1972), 46. For more on this point, see Joan Hoff Wilson, "Herbert Hoover's Plan for Ending the Second World War," *The International History Review* 1 (Jan. 1979), 84-102.

Herbert Hoover: A Select Bibliography

Richard Dean Burns

This compilation is drawn, in part, from Burns' *Herbert Hoover: A Bibliography of His Times and Presidency*, soon to appear in Scholarly Resources' Presidential Bibliography Series.

This short bibliography is designed to introduce the researcher to the basic, as well as the most current, writings related to Herbert Hoover's life and his career. Since the emphasis of this volume is on historians' renewed interest in Hoover's ideas and actions, this list is designed to emphasize those writings. The items contained in the "Historiography" segment, located in the "Autobiographies, Biographies & Memoirs" section immediately below, do expand somewhat on the themes introduced in the preceeding historiographical essays. Elsewhere I have introduced other assessments which focus on specific aspects of Hoover ideas and his political endeavors and which offer challenging interpretations. Some of these interpretations suggest a positive view of Hoover's ideas and actions; others are more critical.

The items included in this survey should not be viewed as a definitive list. I am preparing a more comprehensive bibliographical study that focuses on Hoover's life, especially the activities, events and policies of his presidential years.

The bibliography survey below is arranged under subject headings to assist the search for items that relate to specific themes. The initial section introduces the basic Hoover biographical materials, items reviewing his philosophy and locates his speeches, public papers and writings. The second section develops Hoover's early political life, including his World War I relief activities and his service as

Food Administrator, his efforts as Secretary of Commerce, and concludes with materials on his activities during his postpresidential years. The third major section deals with the Hoover presidency and emphasizes the domestic issues it confronted; much less space is devoted to foreign affairs.

AUTOBIOGRAPHIES, BIOGRAPHIES & MEMOIRS

Included in this section are accounts of Hoover's life and activities and his philosophy.

BIOGRAPHIES

Listed here are various biographical studies of Herbert Hoover. George H. Nash's two volumes bring his comprehensive biography of Hoover up to 1917; this series may ultimately reach eight volumes. Meanwhile, a number of fine single volume biographies have appeared in recent years, including those by David Burner, Richard Norton Smith and Joan Hoff Wilson. Additionally, several older biographies identified in the essays above have been included.

Burner, David. *Herbert Hoover: A Public Life.* New York: Knopf, 1979.

Emerson, Edwin. *Hoover and His Times.* Garden City, NY: Garden City Publishing Co., 1932.

Hoover, Herbert C. *Fishing for Fun—And to Wash Your Soul.* Ed. by William Nichols. New York: Random House, 1963.

Hoover, Herbert C. *The Memoirs of Herbert Hoover.* 3 vols. New York: Macmillan, 1951-1952.

Irwin, Will. *Herbert Hoover: A Reminiscent Biography.* New York: Century, 1928.

Joslin, Theodore G. *Hoover Off the Record.* New York: Doubleday, Doran, 1934.

Kennedy, Hugh A. Studdert. *Hoover in 1932.* San Francisco, CA: Farrallon Press, 1932.

Lyons, Eugene. *Our Unknown Ex-President: A Portrait of Herbert Hoover.* Garden City, NY: Doubleday, 1948. (This is the first of three versions to appear from 1948 to 1964)

McGee, Dorothy Horton. *Herbert Hoover: Engineer, Humanitarian, Statesman.* New York: Dodd, Mead, 1959.

Nash, George H. *The Life of Herbert Hoover: The Engineer, 1874-1914*. New York: Norton, 1983.

Nash, George H. *The Life of Herbert Hoover: The Humanitarian, 1914-1917*. New York: Norton, 1988.

Nash, Lee, ed. *Understanding Herbert Hoover: Ten Perspectives*. Stanford, CA: Hoover Institution Press, 1987. (The ten perspectives are those of Joan Hoff Wilson, George H. Nash, Mark O. Hatfield, David Burner, Ellis W. Hawley, Susan Estebrook Kennedy, Gary Dean Best, Frank Freidel, Robert E. Burke, and William G. Robbins.)

Reeves, Earl. *This Man Hoover*. New York: A.L. Burt, 1928.

Robinson, Edgar Eugene and Vaughn Davis Bornet. *Herbert Hoover: President of the United States*. Stanford, CA: Hoover Institution Press, 1975.

Smith, Richard Norton. *An Uncommon Man: The Triumph of Herbert Hoover*. New York: Simon & Schuster, 1984.

Terzian, James P. *The Many Worlds of Herbert Hoover*. New York: Julian Messner, 1966.

Wilson, Carol Green. *Herbert Hoover: A Challenge for Today*. New York: Evans, 1968.

Wilson, Joan Hoff. *Herbert Hoover: Forgotten Progressive*. Boston: Little, Brown, 1975.

Wolfe, Harold. *Herbert Hoover: Public Servant and Leader of the Loyal Opposition*. New York: Exposition Press, 1956.

Wood, Clement. *Herbert Clark Hoover: An American Tragedy*. New York: M. Swain, 1932.

PHILOSOPHY

Hoover's concept of "individualism" and his interest in "efficiency" and "voluntarism" are discussed in works listed here.

Arnold, Peri E. "Herbert Hoover and the Positive State," In David Greenstone, ed., *Public Values and Private Power in American Politics*. Chicago: University of Chicago Press, 1982, pp. 109-138.

Burner, David and Thomas R. West, "A Technocrat's Morality: Conservatism and Hoover the Engineer." In Stanley Elkins and Eric McKitrick, eds., *The Hofstadter Aegis: A Memorial*. New York: Knopf, 1974, pp. 235-256.

Carey, George W. "Herbert Hoover's Concept of Individualism Revisited." In E.W. Hawley, ed. *Herbert Hoover as Secretary of Commerce.* Iowa City: University of Iowa Press, 1981, pp. 217-254.

Dexter, Walter Friar. *Herbert Hoover and American Individualism: A Modern Interpretation of a National Ideal.* New York: Macmillian, 1932.

Eckley, Wilton. *Herbert Hoover.* Boston: Twayne, 1980). (Hoover is viewed as a spokesman for individualism)

Emery, Anne. *American Friend: Herbert Hoover.* Chicago: Rand McNally, 1967.

Hearden, Patrick. "Herbert Hoover and the Dream of Capitalism in One Country." In Lloyd C. Gardner, ed. *Redefining the Past: In Honor of William Appleman Williams.* Corvallis: Oregon State University Press, 1986, pp. 143-155.

Hinshaw, David. *Herbert Hoover: American Quaker.* New York: Farrar, Strauss & Young, 1950.

Hoover, Herbert. *American Individualism.* Garden City, NY: Doubleday, Page, 1922.

Hoover, Herbert. *The Challenge to Liberty.* New York: Scribner's, 1935.

Lohoff, Bruce A. "Herbert Hoover: Spokesman of Humane Efficiency." *American Quarterly* 22 (1970): 690-700.

Nash, George H. "The Social Philosophy of Herbert Hoover." *Annals of Iowa* 45 (1980): 478-496. (reprinted in *Herbert Hoover Reassessed.* Washington, DC: GPO, 1981, pp. 89-102.)

Olson, James S. "The Philosophy of Herbert Hoover: A Contemporary Perspective." *Annals of Iowa* 43 (1976): 149-161.

Rothbard, Murray N. "The Hoover Myth." *Studies on the Left* 4 (1966):70-84. (reprinted in J. Weinstein and D.W.Eakins, eds. *For a New America.* New York: Random House, 1970, pp. 162-179.)

Walsh, Tom. "Herbert Hoover Reassessed? Progressive? Conservative? Radical?" *Ripon Forum* 23 (June 1987)), 12-13.

Williams, William Appleman. *Some Presidents: Wilson to Nixon.* New York: Vintage, 1972. (see ch. 2)

Williams, William Appleman. "The Central Role of Herbert Hoover in the Maturation of an Industrial Gentry." In *The Contours of American History.* Cleveland, OH: World, 1961, pp. 425-438.

HISTORIOGRAPHY

Grouped here are various assessments of Herbert Hoover and his presidency, and the changes in these assessments over the years.

Davis, Joseph S. "Herbert Hoover, 1874-1964: Another Appraisal." *South Atlantic Quarterly* 67 (1969): 295-318.

Hawley, Ellis W. "Secretary Hoover and the Changing Framework of New Era Historiography." In E.W. Hawley, ed. *Herbert Hoover as Secretary of Commerce: Studies in New Era Thought and Practice.* Iowa City: University of Iowa Press, 1981, pp. 1-16.

Herbert Hoover Reassessed: Essays Commemorating the Fiftieth Anniversary of the Inauguration of Our Thirty-first President. Washington, DC: GPO, 1981. (A number of essays had been previously published; but the leading ones that had not been are cited separately under the appropriate subject heading.)

Lee, David D. "The Politics of Less: The Trials of Herbert Hoover and Jimmy Carter." *Presidential Studies Quarterly* 13 (1983): 305-312.

McCoy, Donald R. "Trends in Viewing Herbert Hoover, Franklin Delano Roosevelt, Harry S. Truman, and Dwight D. Eisenhower." *Midwest Quarterly* 29 (1979): 117-136.

Noggle, Burl. "The Twenties: A New Historiographical Frontier." *Journal of American History* 53 (1966): 299-314.

Wilson, Joan Hoff. "Herbert Hoover Reassessed." In *Herbert Hoover Reassessed.* Washington, DC: GPO, 1981, pp. 103-119.

Wilson, Joan Hoff. "Herbert Hoover: The Popular Image of an Unpopular President." In Lee Nash, ed. *Understanding Herbert Hoover.* Stanford,CA: Hoover Institution Press, 1987, pp. 3-23.

Zieger, Robert H. "Herbert Hoover: A Reinterpretation." *American Historical Review* 81 (1976): 800-810.

SPEECHES AND WRITING

For additional Hoover writings, and he was prolific, see Kathleen Tracey, comp. *Herbert Hoover—A Bibliography: His Writings and His Addresses.* Stanford, CA: Hoover Institution Press, 1977.

Hoover, Herbert C. *Hoover After Dinner.* New York: Scribner's, 1933.

Hoover, Herbert. *Addresses Upon the American Road, 1938-1960.* 8 vols. New York & elsewhere: C. D. Van Nostrand, Standford University Press, Caxton, 1938-1961.

Hoover, Herbert and Calvin Coolidge. *Campaign Speeches of 1932.* Garden City, NY: Doubleday, Doran, 1932.

Hoover, Herbert C. *The New Day: Campaign Speeches of Herbert Hoover, 1928.* Stanford, CA: Stanford University Press, 1928.

Myers, William Starr. *The State Papers and Other Public Writings of Herbert Hoover.* 2 vols. New York: Doubleday, Doran, 1934.

Public Papers of the Presidents of the United States: Herbert Hoover, 1929-1933. 4 vols. Washington: GPO, 1974-1977.

HOOVER'S POLITICAL LIFE

Works listed below range from studies of Hoover's early life to his postpresidential years. Exempted are those accounts dealing with his presidency, which are listed in the subsequent section.

GENERAL

Cornwall, Elmer E., Jr. "Retrogresson: Hoover." In *Presidential Leadership of Public Opinion.* Bloomington: Indiana University Press, 1965, pp. 99-114. (negative)

Hard, William. *Who's Hoover?* New York: Dodd, Mead, 1928.

THE EARLY YEARS

Blainey, Geoffrey. "Herbert Hoover's Forgotten Years." *Business Archives and History* 3 (1963): 53-70. (Hoover's Australian mining experiences)

Hoover, Herbert. *A Boyhood in Iowa.* New York: Aventine Press, 1931.

Johnson, James P. "Herbert Hoover and David Copperfield: A Tale of Two Childhoods." *Journal of Psychohistory* 7 (1980): 467-475.

Johnson, James P. "Herbert Hoover: The Orphan as Children's Friend." *Prologue* 12 (1980): 193-206.

Nash, George H. *Herbert Hoover and Stanford University.* Stanford, CA: Hoover Institution Press, 1988.

WORLD WAR I AND AFTERMATH

Hoover's service as President Wilson's Food Administrator and his direction of "relief" activities are emphasized here.

Best, Gary Dean. "The Hoover-for-President Boom of 1920." *Mid-America* 53 (1971): 227-244.

Best, Gary Dean. *The Politics of American Individualism: Herbert Hoover in Transition, 1918-1921*. Westport, CT: Greenwood, 1975.

Gelfand, Lawrence E., ed. *Herbert Hoover: The Great War and Its Aftermath, 1914-1923*. Iowa City: University of Iowa Press, 1979.

Himmelberg, Robert F. "Hoover's Public Image, 1919-1920: The Emergence of a Public Figure and a Sign of the Times." In L. E. Gelfand, ed. *Herbert Hoover: The Great War and Its Aftermath*. Iowa City: University of Iowa Press, 1979, pp. 207-232.

Hoover, Herbert. *America's First Crusade*. New York: Scribner's, 1942.

O'Brien, Francis W., ed. *The Hoover-Wilson Wartime Correspondence: September 24, 1914 to November 11, 1918*. Ames, IA: Iowa State University Press, 1974.

O'Brien, Francis W., ed. *Two Peacemakers in Paris: The Hoover-Wilson Post-Armistice Letters*. College Station: Texas A&M University Press, 1978.

Schmidt, Royal J. "Hoover's Reflections on the Versailles Treaty." In L.E. Gelfand, ed. *Herbert Hoover: Great War and Its Aftermath*. Iowa City: University of Iowa Press, 1979, pp. 61-86.

Food Administrator

Best, Gary Dean. "Food Relief as Price Support: Hoover and American Pork, January-March 1919." *Agricultural History* 45 (1971): 49-84.

Best, Gary Dean. "Herbert Hoover's Technical Mission to Yugoslavia, 1919-1920." *Annals of Iowa* 42 (1974): 443-459.

Cuff, Robert D. "Herbert Hoover, the Ideology of Voluntarism and War Organization During the Great War." *Journal of American History* 64 (1977): 358-372. (Reprinted in L.E. Gelfand, *Herbert Hoover: Great War and Its Aftermath*)

Cuff, Robert D. "The Dilemmas of Voluntarism: Hoover and the Pork-Packing Agreement of 1917-1919." *Agricultural History* 53 (1979): 727-747.

Guth, James L. "Herbert Hoover, the U.S. Food Administration and the Dairy Industry." *Business History Review* 55 (1981): 170-187.

Hall, Tom G. "Government Controls: How to Understand the Experience of World War I." In Trudy H. Peterson, ed., *Farmers,*

Bureaucrats and Middlemen. Washington, DC: Howard University Press, 1980, pp. 279-295.

Sworakowski, Witold S. "Herbert Hoover, Launching the American Food Administration." In L.E. Gelfand, ed. *Herbert Hoover: Great War and Its Aftermath.* Iowa City: University of Iowa Press, 1979, pp. 40-60.

Winters, Donald D. "The Hoover-Wallace Controversy During World War I." *Annals of Iowa* 39 (1969): 586-597.

Relief

Hoover, Herbert. *An American Epic.* 4 vols. Chicago: Regnery, 1959-1960.

Lambert, C. Roger. "Food from the Public Crib: Agricultural Surpluses and Food Relief Under Herbert Hoover." In C.E. Krog and W.R. Tanner, eds. *Herbert Hoover and the Republican Era: A Reconsideration.* Lanham, MD: University Press of America, 1984, pp. 157-190.

Lambert, C. Roger. "Hoover, the Red Cross and Food for the Hungry." *Annals of Iowa* 44 (1979): 530-540.

Rothbard, Murray N. "Hoover's 1919 Food Diplomacy in Retrospect." In L.E. Gelfand, ed. *Herbert Hoover: Great War and Its Aftermath.* Iowa City: University of Iowa Press, 1979, pp. 87-110. (very critical)

Weissman, Benjamin. *Herbert Hoover and Famine Relief to Soviet Russia, 1921-1923.* Stanford, CA: Hoover Institution Press, 1974. (a brief summary of this episode appears in *Herbert Hoover Reassessed.* Washington, DC; G.P.O., 1981, pp. 390-396)

Willis, Edward F. "Herbert Hoover and the Blockade of Germany, 1918-1919." In Frederick J. Cox, et al., ed. *Studies in Modern European History in Honor of Franklin Charles Palm.* New York: Bookman Assoc., 1956, pp. 265-310.

Willis, Edward F. *Herbert Hoover and the Russian Prisoners of World War I: A Study in Diplomacy and Relief, 1918-1919.* Stanford, CA: Stanford University Press, 1951.

SECRETARY OF COMMERCE

Hoover was an exceptionally active member of the Harding and Coolidge cabinets. He sought to link government and business through voluntary associations which would define and further the joint interests of both groups.

Books & Dissertations

Arnold, Peri E. "Herbert Hoover and the Department of Commerce: A Study in Ideology and Policy." Ph.D. dissertation, University of Chicago, 1972.

Brandes, Joseph. *Herbert Hoover and Economic Diplomacy: Department of Commerce Policy, 1921-1928*. Pittsburgh, PA: University of Pittsburgh Press, 1962.

Hawley, Ellis W., ed. *Herbert Hoover as Secretary of Commerce, 1921-1928: Studies in New Era Thought and Practice*. Iowa City: University of Iowa Press, 1981.

Hogan, Michael J. *Informal Entente: The Private Structure of Cooperation in Anglo-American Economic Diplomacy, 1918-1928*. Columbia: University of Missouri Press, 1977.

Parrini, Carl P. *Heir to Empire: United States Economic Diplomacy, 1916-1923*. Pittsburgh: University of Pittsburgh Press, 1969.

Rosen, Philip T. *The Modern Stentors: Radio Broadcasters and the Federal Government, 1920-1934*. Westport: Greenwood, 1980.

Essays

Best, Gary Dean. "President Wilson's Second Industrial Conference." *Labor History* 16 (1975): 505-520.

Drake, Douglas C. "Herbert Hoover, Ecologist: The Politics of Oil Pollution Control, 1921-1926." *Mid-America* 55 (1973): 207-228.

Grin, Carolyn. "The Unemployment Conference of 1921: An Experiment in National Cooperative Planning." *Mid-America* 55 (1973):83-107.

Hawley, Ellis W. "Herbert Hoover, the Commerce Secretariat, and the Vision of an 'Associative State,' 1921-1928." *Journal of American History* 61 (1974): 116-140.

Hawley, Ellis W. "Secretary Hoover and the Bitumonious Coal Problem, 1921-28." *Business History Review* 42 (1968): 247-270.

Hawley, Ellis. "Three Facets of Hooverian Associationalism: Lumber, Aviation, and Movies, 1921-1930." In Thomas K. McCraw, ed., *Regulation in Perspective: Historical Essays*. Boston: Harvard Business School, 1981.

Hogan, Michael J. "Informal Entente: Public Policy and Private Management in Anglo-American Petroleum Affairs." *Business History Review* 48 (1974): 187-205.

Koerselman, Gary H. "Secretary Hoover and National Farm Policy: Problems of Leadership." *Agricultural History* 51 (1977): 378-395.

Lee, David D. "Herbert Hoover and the Development of Commercial Aviation, 1921-1926." *Business History Review* 58 (1984): 78-102.

Leffler, Melvyn P. "Herbert Hoover, the 'New Era,' and American Foreign Policy, 1921-29." In E.W. Hawley, *Herbert Hoover as Secretary of Commerce*. Iowa City: University of Iowa Press, 1981, pp. 148-182.

Lohof, Bruce A. "Herbert Hoover, Spokesman of Humane Efficiency: The Mississippi Flood of 1927." *American Quarterly* 22 (1970): 690-700.

Metcalf, Evan B. "Secretary Hoover and the Emergence of Macroeconomic Management." *Business History Review* 49 (1975): 60-80.

Meter, Robert H., Jr. "Herbert Hoover and the Economic Reconstruction of Europe." In L.E.Gelfand, ed. *Hebert Hoover: Great War and Its Aftermath*. Iowa City: University of Iowa Press, 1979, pp. 143-181.

Wilson, Joan Hoff. "Hoover's Agricultural Policies, 1921-1928." *Agricultural History* 51 (1977): 335-361.

Zieger, Robert H. "Herbert Hoover, the Wage-Earner and the "New Economic System, 1919-29." In E.W. Hawley, ed. *Herbert Hoover as Secretary of Commerce*. Iowa City: University of Iowa Press, 1981, pp.82-112.

Zieger, Robert H. "Solving the Labor Problem: Herbert Hoover and the American Worker in the 1920s." In *Herbert Hoover Reassessed*. Washington, DC: GPO, 1981, pp. 177-187.

THE POST-PRESIDENTIAL YEARS

Only a portion of Hoover activities after he left the presidency are examined in the works below. He was especially a critic of the New Deal and of U.S. foreign policy during the 1940s and early 1950s.

Best, Gary Dean. "Herbert Hoover as Titular Leader of the GOP, 1933-35." *Mid-America* 61 (1979): 81-97.

Best, Gary Dean. *Herbert Hoover: The Post-Presidential Years, 1933-1964.* 2 Vols. Stanford, CA: Hoover Institution Press, 1983.

As New Deal Critic

Best, Gary Dean. "Herbert Hoover and Postwar Foreign Policy, 1942-1945." In T.T. Thalken, ed. *The Problems of Lasting Peace Revisited.* West Branch, IA: Herbert Hoover Presidential Library Assoc., 1986, pp. 29-50.

Best, Gary Dean "Herbert Hoover, 1933-1941: A Reassessment." In *Herbert Hoover Reassessed.* Washington, D.C.: GPO, 1981, pp. 227-274.

Wilson, Joan Hoff. "Herbert Hoover's Plan for Ending the Second World War." *International History Review* 1 (1979): 84-102.

Wilson, Joan Hoff. "Herbert Hoover's Progressive Response to the New Deal." In John N. Schacht, ed. *Three Progressives from Iowa.* Iowa City: Center for the Study of the Recent History of the United States, 1980, pp. 17-35.

As Foreign Policy Critic

Best, Gary Dean. "Totalitarianism or Peace: Herbert Hoover and the Road to War, 1939-1941. *Annals of Iowa* 44 (1977): 516-529.

Hoover, Herbert and Hugh Gibson. *The Basis of Lasting Peace.* New York: D. Van Nostrand, 1945.

Hoover, Herbert and Hugh Gibson. *The Problem of Lasting Peace.* Garden City, NY: Doubleday, Doran, 1942.

McCoy, Donald R. "Herbert Hoover and Foreign Policy, 1939-1945." In *Herbert Hoover Reassessed.* Washington, DC: GPO, 1981, pp. 401-425.

Mrozek, Donald J. "Progressive Dissenter: Herbert Hoover's Opposition to Truman's Overseas Military Policy." *Annals of Iowa* 43 (1976): 275-291.

Wilson, Joan Hoff. "The Postwar World According to Hoover." In T.T. Thalken, ed. *The Problems of a Lasting Peace Revisited.* West Branch, IA: Herbert Hoover Presidential Library Assoc., 1986, 51-78.

THE HOOVER COMMISIONS (1948/1955)

Arnold, Peri E. *Making the Managerial Presidency: Comprehensive Reorganization Planning, 1905-1980.* Princeton, NJ: Princeton University Press, 1986.

Arnold, Peri E. "The First Hoover Commission and the Managerial Presidency." *Journal of Politics* 38 (1976): 46-70.

Moe, Ronald C. *The Hoover Commissions Revisited.* Boulder, CO: Westview, 1982.

Pemberton, William E. *Bureaucratic Politics: Executive Reorganization during the Truman Administration.* Columbia: University of Missouri Press, 1979.

THE HOOVER PRESIDENCY

As the essays above have indicated there has been much renewed interest in Hoover's policies and activities as president, especially his responses to the onset of the depression. Many of Hoover's presidential policies have roots in his activities as Secretary of Commerce; therefore, one is advised to review that section as well as the segments below.

OVERVIEWS

These accounts relate to the interwar decades, especially the 1920s, and are included because they provide the background against which the Hoover presidency is weighted. Books and essays have been separated for ease of scanning.

Books

Barber, William J. *From New Era to New Deal: Herbert Hoover, the Economists, and American Economic Policy, 1921-1933.* New York: Cambridge University Press, 1985.

Burner, David. *The Politics of Provincialism: The Democratic Party in Transition, 1918-1932.* New York: Knopf, 1968.

Hawley, Ellis W. *The Great War and the Search for Modern Order: A History of the American People and Their Institutions, 1917-1933.* New York: St. Martin's, 1979,

Hicks, John D. *Republican Ascendency, 1921-1933.* New York: Harper, 1960.

Johnson, Walter. *1600 Pennsylvania Avenue: Presidents and the People, 1929-1959*. Boston: Little, Brown, 1960.

Leuchtenberg, William E. *The Perils of Prosperity, 1914-1932*. Chicago: University of Chicago Press, 1958.

McCoy, Donald R. *Coming of Age: The United States during the 1920's and 1930's*. Baltimore, MD: Penguin, 1973.

Mowry, George E. *The Urban Nation, 1920-1960*. New York: Hill & Wang, 1965.

Schlesinger, Arthur Jr. *The Crisis of the Old Order, 1919-1933*. Boston: Houghton Mifflin, 1957.

Schriftgiesser, Karl. *This Was Normalcy: An Account of Party Politics During Twelve Republican Years, 1920-1932*. Boston: Little Brown, 1948.

Shannon, David A. *Between the Wars: America, 1919-1941*. Boston: Houghton Mifflin, 1979.

Essays

Arnold, Peri. "Herbert Hoover and the Continuity of American Public Policy [1921-1933]." *Public Policy* 20 (1972): 525-544.

Hawley, Ellis W. "'Industrial Policy' in the 1920s and 1930s." In Claude Barfield and William Schambra, eds. *The Politics of Industrial Policy*. Washington, DC: American Enterprise Institute, 1986, pp. 63-86.

Himmelberg, Robert F. "Government and Business, 1917-1932." In Joseph Frese and Jacob Judd, eds. *Business and Government: Essays in 20th Century Cooperation and Confrontation*. Tarrytown, NY: Sleepy Hollow Press, 1985, pp. 1-23.

Kollock, Will. "The Story of a Friendship: Mark Sullivan and Herbert Hoover." *Pacific Historian* 18 (1974): 31-48.

Link, Arthur S. "What Happened to the Progressive Movement in the 1920's?" *American Historical Review* 64 (1959): 833-851.

McQuaid, Kim. "Corporate Liberalism in the American Business Community, 1920-1940." *Business History Review* 52 (1978): 342-368.

Williams, William Appleman. "The Central Role of Herbert Hoover in the Maturation of an Industrial Gentry." In *The Contours of American History*. Cleveland, OH: World, 1961, pp. 425-438.

ADMINISTRATION & POLITICS

Books

Alchon, Guy. *The Invisible Hand of Planning: Capitalism, Social Science, and the State in the 1920s.* Princeton, NJ: Princeton University Press, 1985.

Crowther, Samuel. *The Presidency vs. Hoover.* New York: Doubleday, Dorn, 1928.

Fausold, Martin L. and Mazuzan, George T., eds. *The Hoover Presidency: A Reappraisal.* Albany: State University of New York Press, 1974.

Fausold, Martin L. *The Presidency of Herbert C. Hoover.* Lawrence: University Press of Kansas, 1985.

Hawley, Ellis W.; Himmelberg, Robert F.; Nash, Gerald D.; and Rothbard, Murray N. *Herbert Hoover and the Crisis of American Capitalism.* Cambridge: Schenkman, 1973.

Krog, Carl E. and William R. Tanner, eds., *Herbert Hoover and the Republican Era: A Reconsideraion.* Lanham, Md.: University Press of America, 1984. Included were essays on Hoover's anti-waste campaign (Tanner), aviation program (David D. Lee), recreational policies (Krog), Indian reforms (William G. Robbins), racial attitudes (Larry Grothaus), agricultural programs (C. Roger Lambert and Bernard M. Klass), and relations with Gerald P. Nye (David A. Horowitz).

Lloyd, Craig. *Aggresive Introvert: A Study of Herbert Hoover and Public Relations Management, 1912-1932.* Columbus: Ohio State University Press, 1972.

Marsh, William J., Jr. *Our President Herbert Hoover.* Garden City, NY: Doubleday, Doran, 1930.

Myers, William Starr, and Walter H. Newton. *The Hoover Administration: A Documented Narrative.* New York: Scribner's, 1936.

Schwarz, Jordan A. *The Interregnum of Despair: Hoover, Congress, and the Depression.* Urbana: University of Illinois Press, 1970.

Wilbur, Ray Lyman and Arthur Mastick Hyde. *The Hoover Policies.* New York: Scribner's, 1937.

Essays

Arnold, Peri E. "The 'Great Engineer' as Administrator: Herbert Hoover and Modern Bureaucracy." *Review of Politics* 42 (1980): 328-348.

Burner, David. "Before the Crash: Hoover's First Eight Months in the Presidency." In M.L. Fausold and G.T. Mazuzan, eds.. *The Hoover Presidency: A Reappraisal*. Albany: State University of New York Press, 1974, pp. 50-65.

Degler, Carl. "The Ordeal of Herbert Hoover." *Yale Review* 52 (1963): 563-583.

Freidel, Frank, Jr. "Hoover and Roosevelt and Historical Continuity." In *Herbert Hoover Reassessed*. Washington, DC: GPO, 1981, pp. 275-291.

Ginzl, David J. "The Politics of Patronage: Florida Republicans during the Hoover Administration." *Florida Historical Quarterly*, 61 (1982): 1-19.

Hargrove, Erwin C. "Herbert Hoover: The Engineer." In *Presidential Leadership: Personality and Political Style*. New York: Macmillan, 1966, pp. 97-117. (questions Hoover's political skills as president)

Hawley, Elis W. "Herbert Hoover and American Corporatism, 1929-1933." In M.L. Fausold and G.T. Mazuzan, eds. *The Hoover Presidency: A Reappraisal*. Albany: State University of New York Press, 1974, pp. 101-119.

Hawley, Ellis W. "Herbert Hoover, 1929-1933." In Frank N. Magill and John L. Loos, eds. *The American Presidents: The Office and the Men*. Pasadena. CA: Salem Press, 1986, pp. 555-574.

Hofstadter, Richard. *"Herbert Hoover and the Crisis of American Indidualism."* In *The American Political Tradition and the Men Who Made It*. New York: Knopf, 1948, pp. 281-314.

Karl, Barry D. "Presidential Planning and Social Science Research: Mr. Hoover's Experts." *Perspectives in American History* 3 (1969): 347-409.

Karl, Barry D. "The Social Sciences and Mr. Hoover: Recent Social Trends." In his *Charles E. Merriam and the Study of Politics*. Chicago: University of Chicago Press, 1974, pp. 201-225.

Krock, Arthur. "President Hoover's Two Years." *Current History* 34 (1931): 488-494.

Nevins, Allan. "President Hoover's Record." *Current History* 36 (1932):385-394.

Schwarz, Jordan A. "Hoover and Congress: Politics, Personality, and Perspective." In M.L. Fausold and G.T. Mazuzan, eds. *The Hoover Presidency: A Reappraisal.* Albany: State University of New York Press, 1974, pp. 87-100.

Stevens, Susan. "The Congressional Elections of 1930: Politics of Avoidance." In Milton Plesur, ed. *An American Historian: Essays to Honor Selig Adler.* Buffalo: State University of New York Press, 1980, pp. 149-158.

Wilson, John. "The Quaker and the Sword: Herbert Hoover's Relations with the Military." *Military Affairs* 37 (1974): 41-47.

AGRICULTURE & CONSERVATION

Clements, Kendrick A. "Herbert Hoover and the Fish." *Journal of Psychohistory* 10 (1983): 333-348.

Clements, Kendrick. "Herbert Hoover and Conservation, 1921-1933." *American Historical Review* 89 (1984): 67-88.

Edwards, John C. "Herbert Hoover's Public Lands Policy: A Struggle for Control." *Pacific Historian* 20 (1976): 34-45.

Fausold, Martin L. "President Hoover's Farm Policies, 1929-1933." *Agricultural History* 51 (1977): 362-377.

Hamilton, David E. "From New Era to New Deal: American Farm Policy Between the Wars." In Lawrence Gelfand and Robert Neymeyer, eds. *Agricultural Distress and the Midwest: Past and Present.* Iowa City: Center for the Study of the Recent History of the United States, 1986, pp. 19-54.

Hamilton, David E. "Herbert Hoover and the Great Drought of 1930:" *Journal of American History* 68 (1982): 850-875.

Klass, Bernard M. "The Federal Farm Board and the Antecedents of the Agricultural Adjustment Act, 1929-1933." In C.E. Krog and W.R. Tanner, eds. *Herbert Hoover and the Republican Era: A Reconsideration.* Lanham, MD: University Press of America, 1984, pp. 191-219.

Krog, Carl. "'Organizing the Production of Leisure:' Herbert Hoover and the Conservation movements of the 1920s," *Wisconsin Magazine of History* 67 (1984): 199-218.

Johnson, William R. "Herbert Hoover and the Regulation of Grain Futures." *Mid-America* 51 (1969): 155-174.

Robbins, William G. "Voluntary Cooperation v. Regulatory Paternalism: The Lumber Trade in the 1920s." *Business History Review* 56 (1982): 358-379.

Shideler, James H. "Herbert Hoover and the Federal Farm Board Project." *Mississippi Valley Historical Review* 42 (1956): 717-729.

Swain, Donald O. *Federal Conservation Policy, 1921-1933*. Berkeley: University of California Press, 1963.

Woodruff, Nan Elizabeth. *As Rare as Rain: Federal Relief in the Great Southern Drought of 1930-1931*. Champaign: University of Illinois Press, 1985.

BUSINESS, TRADE & TRANSPORTATION

Himmelberg, Robert F. "President Hoover, Organized Business, and the Antitrust Laws: A Study in Hooverian Ideology and Policy." In *Herbert Hoover Reassessed*. Washington, DC: GPO, 1981, pp. 123-144.

Hubbard, Preston. Jr., *Origins of the TVA*. Nashville, TN: Vanderbilt University Press, 1961.

Kottman, Richard N. "Herbert Hoover and the St. Lawrence Seaway Treaty of 1932." *New York History* 56 (1975): 315-347.

Snyder, J. Richard. "Hoover and the Hawley-Smoot Tariff: A View of Executive Leadership." *Annals of Iowa* 41 (1973): 1173-1189.

Wiebe, Robert H. *Businessmen and Reform*. Cambridge: Harvard University Press, 1962.

FINANCE & LABOR

Kennedy, Susan Estabrook. *The Banking Crisis of 1933*. Lexington: University Press of Kentucky, 1973. (see chs. 2-6)

Olson, James S. "Rehersal for Disaster: Hoover, the RFC, and the Banking Crisis in Nevada, 1932-1933." *Western Historical Quarterly* 6 (1975): 149-161.

Olson, James S. "The End of Voluntarism: Herbert Hoover and the National Credit Corporation." *Annals of Iowa* 41 (1972): 104-113.

Zieger, Robert H. "Herbert Hoover, the Wage Earner, and the 'New Economic System,' 1919-1929." *Business History Review* 51 (1977): 161-189.

Zieger, Robert H. "Labor, Progressivism, and Herbert Hoover in the 1920's." *Wisconsin Magazine of History* 58 (1975): 196-208.

Zieger, Robert H. *Republicans and Labor, 1919-1929.* Lexington: University of Kentucky Press, 1969.

THE DEPRESSION (CAUSES & REACTIONS)

Berkowitz, Edward D. and Kim McQuaid. "Bureaucrats as 'Social Engineers': Federal Welfare Programs in Herbert Hoover's America." *American Journal of Economics and Sociology* 39 (1980): 321-335.

Daniels, Roger. *The Bonus March: An Episode of the Great Depression.* Westport, CT: Greenwood, 1941.

Himmelberg, Robert F. "Herbert Hoover and the Great Depression." In Philip C. Dolce and George H. Skau, eds. *Power and the Presidency.* New York: Scribner's 1976, pp. 88-100.

Lambert, C. Roger. "Hoover, the Red Cross and Food for the Hungry." *Annals of Iowa* 44 (1978): 530-540.

Lambert, C. Roger. "Hoover and the Red Cross in the Arkansas Drought of 1930." *Arkansas Historical Quarterly* 29 (1970): 3-19.

Lisio, Donald J. *The President and Protest: Hoover, Conspiracy, and the Bonus Riot.* Columbia: University of Missouri Press, 1974.

McElvaine, Robert S. *The Great Depression: America, 1929-1941.* New York: Times Books, 1984. (see ch. 3)

Meltzer, Milton. *Brother, Can You Spare a Dime? The Great Depression, 1929-1933.* New York: Knopf, 1969.

Mitchell, Broadus. *Depression Decade.* New York: Holt, Rinehart, 1947.

Mullins, William H. "Self Help in Seattle, 1931-32: Herbert Hoover's Concept of Cooperative Individualism and the Unemployed Citizen's League." *Pacific Northwest Quarterly* 72 (1981): 11-19.

Ortquist, Richard T. "Unemployment and Relief: Michigan's Response to the Depression During the Hoover Years." *Michigan History* 57 (1973):209-236.

Romasco, Albert U. *The Poverty of Abundance: Hoover, the Nation, the Depression.* New York: Oxford University Press, 1965.

Rosen, Elliot A. *Hoover, Roosevelt, and the Brains Trust: From Depression to New Deal.* New York: Columbia University Press, 1977.

Rothbard, Murray N. *America's Great Depression.* Princeton, NJ: D. Van Nostrand, 1963.

Smith, Gene. *The Shattered Dream: Herbert Hoover and the Great Depression*. New York: William Morrow, 1970.

Warren, Harris G. *Herbert Hoover and the Great Depression*. New York: Oxford University Press, 1959.

Wecter, Dixon. *The Age of the Great Depression, 1929-1941*. New York: Macmillian, 1948.

Whisenhunt, Donald W. *The Depression in Texas: The Hoover Years*. New York: Garland, 1983.

A Prelude to the New Deal?

Arnold, Peri E. "Herbert Hoover and the Continuity of American Public Policy." *Public Policy* 20 (1972): 525-544.

Brinkley, Alan. "The New Deal: Prelude." *Wilson Quarterly* 6 (1982): 50-61.

Freidel, Frank Jr. "Hoover and Roosevelt and Historical Continuity." In *Herbert Hoover Reassessed*. Washington, DC: GPO, 1981, pp. 275-291.

Freidel, Frank "The Interregnum Struggle Between Hoover and Roosevelt." In M.L. Fausold and G.T. Mazuzan, eds. *The Hoover Presidency: A Reappraisal*. Albany: State University of New York Press, 1974, pp. 134-149.

Himmelberg, Robert F. *The Origins of the National Recovery Administration: Business, Government and the Trade Association Issue, 1921-1933*. New York: Fordham University Press, 1976.

Nash, Gerald D. "Herbert Hoover and the Origins of the Reconstruction Finance Corporation." *Mississippi Valley Historical Review* 46 (1959): 455-468.

Olson, James S. *Herbert Hoover and the Reconstruction Finance Corporation, 1931-1933*. Ames: Iowa State University Press, 1977.

Romasco, Albert U. "Herbert Hoover's Policies for Dealing with the Great Depression: The End of the Old Order or the Beginning of the New?" In M. Fausold and G. Mazuzan, eds. *The Hoover Presidency: A Reappraisal*. Albany: State University of New York Press, 1974, pp. 69-86.

Sautter, Udo. "Government and Unemployment: The Use of Public Works before the New Deal." *Journal of American History* 73 (1986): 59-86.

SOCIAL REFORM

Berkowitz. Edward D. and Kim McQuaid. "Bureaucrats as Social Engineers: Federal Welfare Programs in Herbert Hoover's America." *American Journal of Economics and Sociology 39* (1980): 321-335.

Bornet, Vaughn Davis. "Herbert Hoover's Planning for Unemployment and Old Age Insurance Coverage, 1921 to 1933." In John N. Schacht, ed., *The Quest for Security: Papers on the Origins and the Future of the American Social Insurance System.* Iowa City: Center for the Study of the Recent History of the United States, 1982, pp. 35-71.

Giglio, James N. "Voluntarism and Public Policy Between World War I and the New Deal: Herbert Hoover and the American Child Health Association." *Presidential Studies Quarterly* 13 (1983): 430-452.

MINORITIES

Day, David S. "Herbert Hoover and Racial Politics: The DePriest Incident." *Journal of Negro History* 65 (1980): 6-17.

Garcia, George F. "Black Disaffection from the Republican Party during the Presidency of Herbert Hoover, 1928-1932." *Annals of Iowa* 45 (1980): 462-497.

Garcia, George F. "Herbert Hoover and the Issue of Race." *Annals of Iowa* 44 (1979): 507-517.

Ginzl, David J. "Lily-Whites versus Black-and-Tans: Mississippi Republicans during the Hoover Administration." *Journal of Mississippi History* 62 (1980): 194-211.

Ginzl, David J. "Patronage, Race, and Politics: Georgia Republicans During the Hoover Administration." *Georgia Historical Quarterly* 64 (1980): 280-293.

Grothaus, Larry. "Herbert Hoover and Black Americas." In C.E. Krog and W.R. Tanner, eds. *Herbert Hoover and the Republican Era: A Reconisderation.* Lanham, MD: University Press of America, 1984, pp. 120-158.

Lisio, Donald J. *Hoover, Blacks, & Lily-Whites: A Study in Southern Strategies.* Chapel Hill: University of North Carolina Press, 1985.

Philip, Kenneth. "Herbert Hoover's New Era: a False Dawn for the American Indian." *Rocky Mountain Social Science Journal* 9 (1972): 53-60.

Robbins, William G. "Herbert Hoover's Indian Reformers under Attack: The Failures of Administrative Reform." *Mid-America* 63 (1981): 157-170. (reprinted in C.E. Krog and W.R. Tanner, eds. *Herbert Hoover and the Republican Era: A Reconsideration.* Lanham, MD: University Press of America, 1984, pp. 95-119)

EVALUATION

In the Schlesinger polls of 1948 and 1962, Hoover had ranked respectively twentieth and nineteenth. Nor did Murray and Blessing think that Hoover's standing was likely to rise in the future, primarily because they found that younger historians rated him lower than older ones. They did not, however, a wide divergence of judgement among the polled, one that made him the third-most controversial of the presidents and might possibly indicate that a change was underway.

Amlund, Curtis A. "Presidential-Ranking: A Criticism." *Midwest Journal of Political Science* 8 (1964):309-313. (measurable factors are lacking)

Bailey, Thomas A. *Presidential Greatness: The Image and the Man from George Washington to the Present.* New York: Appleton-Century, 1966.

Maranell, Gary M. "The Evaluation of Presidents: An Extension of the Schlesinger Polls." *Journal of American History* 57 (1970): 104-113.

Murray, Robert K. and Tim H. Blessing. "The Presidential Performance Study: A Progress Report." *Journal of American History* 70 (1983): 535-555.

Rossiter, Clinton. "The Presidents and the Presidency." *American Heritage* 7 (Apr. 1965): 28-33, 94.

Schlesinger, Arthur M., Sr. "Our Presidents: A Rating by 75 Historians." *New York Times Magazine,* 29 July 1962, p. 12.

Schlesinger, Arthur M., Sr. "The U.S. Presidents." *Life* 25 (1948): 65-74.

"SMEAR BOOKS"

These scurrilous books, which appeared during the 1932 presidential campaign, questioned Hoover's honest and intregity.

Corey, Herbert. *The Truth About Hoover.* Boston: Houghton Miflin, 1932. (refutes smear charges)

Hamill, John. *The Strange Career of Mr. Hoover Under Two Flags.* New York: William Faro, 1931.

Heaton, John L. *Tough Luck: Hoover Again*. New York: Vanguard, 1932.

Knox, John. *The Great Mistake*. Washington: National Foundation Press, 1932.

Liggett, Walter W. *The Rise of Herbert Hoover*. New York: H. K. Fly, 1932.

Marsh, William J., Jr. and Charles Marsh. *Why You Should Vote for President Hoover*. New York: Norman W. Henley, 1932.

O'Brien, James. *Hoover's Millions and How He Made Them*. New York: O'Brien, 1932.

Sizer, Rosanne. "Herbert Hoover and the Smear Books." *Annals of Iowa* 47 (1984): 343-361.

Train, Arthur. *The Strange Attacks on Herbert Hoover: A Current Example of What We Do to Our Presidents*. New York: John Day, 1932.

HOOVER AND FOREIGN AFFAIRS

While the effects of the Depression carried over into foreign policy issues, there were other factors that also affected foreign affairs—such as, prohibition, Japanese expansionism, and disarmament efforts.

GENERAL

For Hoover's views regarding foreign affairs during and immediately after World War II, see above, "As Foreign Policy Critic."

Books

Current, Richard N. *Secretary Stimson: A Study in Statescraft*. New Brunswick, NJ: Rutgers University Press, 1954.

Ellis, L. Ethan. *Republican Foreign Policy, 1921-1933*. New Brunswick, NJ: Rutgers University Press, 1968.

Ferrell, Robert H. *American Diplomacy in the Great Depression: Hoover-Stimson Foreign Policy, 1929-1933*. New Haven, CT: Yale University Press, 1957.

Myers, William Starr. *The Foreign Policies of Herbert Hoover, 1929-1933*. New York: Scribner's, 1940.

Wilson, Joan Hoff. *American Business and Foreign Policy, 1920-1933*. Lexington: University of Kentucky Press, 1971.

Essays

Adler, Selig. "Hoover's Foreign Policy and the New Left." In M.L. Fausold and G.T. Mazuzan, eds. *The Hoover Presidency: A Reappraisal*. Albany: State University of New York Press, 1974, pp. 153-163.

Blanks, William D. "Herbert Hoover and the Holy Land: A Preliminary Study Based upon Documentary Sources in the Hoover Presidential Library." In Moshe Davis, ed. *With Eyes Toward Zion*. New York: Arno, 1977, pp. 163-172.

Current, Richard N. "The Stimson Doctrine and the Hoover Doctrine." *American Historical Review* 59 (1954): 531-542.

DeBoe, David C. "Secretary Stimson and the Kellop-Briand Pact." In Margaret F. Morris and Sandra L. Myers, eds. *Essays on American Foreign Policy*. Austin: University of Texas Press, 1974, pp. 31-53.

DeConde, Alexander. "Herbert Hoover and Foreign Policy: A Retrospective Assessment." In *Herbert Hoover Reassessment*. Washington, DC: GPO, 1981, pp. 313-334.

Leffler, Melvyn P. "Political Isolationism, Economic Expansion, or Diplomatic Realism." *Perspectives in American History* 8 (1974): 413-461.

Nash, George H. "The Mind of a Peacemaker: The Foundation of Herbert Hoover's World View." In T.T. Thalken, ed. *The Problems of Lasting Peace Revisited*. West Branch, IA: Herbert Hoover Presidential Library Assoc., 1986, pp. 7-28.

Williams, William Appleman. "The Legend of Isolationism in the 1920's." *Science and Society* 18 (1954): 1-20.

Wilson, Joan Hoff. "A Reevaluation of Hoover's Foreign Policy." In M.L. Fausold and G.T. Mazuzan, eds. *The Hoover Presidency: A Reappraisal*. Albany: State University of New York Press, 1974, pp. 165-186.

EAST ASIA

Japan's conquest of Manchuria and the Shanghai Incident were the major incidents affecting U.S.-Asian affairs.

Graebner, Norman A. "Hoover, Roosevelt and the Japanese." In Dorothy Borg and Shumpei Okamoto, eds. *Pearl Harbor as History: Japanese-American Relations, 1931-1941*. New York: Columbia University Press, 1973, pp. 25-52.

Iriye, Akira. "1922-1931." In Ernest R. May and James C. Thomson, Jr., eds. *American-East Asian Relations: A Survey.* Cambridge, MA: Harvard University Press, 1972, pp. 221-259. (historiographical comments on the Manchurian Crisis and the positions of Hoover and Stimson)

Rappaport, Armin. *Henry L. Stimson and Japan, 1931-1933.* Chicago: University of Chicago Press, 1963.

Thorne, Christopher. *The Limits of Foreign Policy: The West, the League, and the Far Eastern Crisis of 1931-1933.* New York: Putnam, 1973.

EUROPE

Bennett, Edward W. *Germany and the Diplomacy of the Financial Crisis, 1931.* Cambridge, MA: Harvard University Press, 1962.

Costigliola, Frank. *Awkward Dominion: American Economic, Political, and Cultural Relations with Europe, 1919-1933.* Ithaca, NY: Cornell University Press, 1984.

Leffler, Melvyn P. *The Elusive Quest: America's Pursuit of European Stability and French Security, 1919-1933.* Chapel Hill: University of North Carolina Press, 1979.

Lochner, Louis P. *Herbert Hoover and Germany.* New York: Macmillan, 1960.

Rodis, Themistocles C. "Russo-American Contacts During the Hoover Administration." *South Atlantic Quarterly* 51 (1952), 235-244.

WESTERN HEMPISHERE

Curry, Earl R. *Hoover's Dominican Diplomacy and the Origins of the Good Neighbor Policy.* New York: Garland, 1979.

DeConde, Alexander. *Herbert Hoover's Latin American Policy.* Stanford, CA: Stanford University Press, 1951.

Kottman, Richard N. "Herbert Hoover and the Smoot-Hawley Tariff: Canada, A Case Study." *Journal of American History* 62 (1975): 609-635.

Kottman, Richard N. "The Hoover-Bennett Meeting of 1931: Mismanaged Summitry." *Annals of Iowa* 42 (1974): 205-221.

INTERNATIONAL ECONOMIC & POLITICS

Accinelli, Robert D. "Hoover Administration and the World Court." *Peace and Change* 4:3 (1977): 28-36.

Christol, Carl Q. "Herbert Hoover: The League of Nations and the World Court." In *Herbert Hoover Reassessed*. Washington, DC: GPO, 1981, pp. 335-379.

Costigliola, Frank. "The Other Side of Isolationism: The Establishment of the First World Bank, 1929-1930." *Journal of American History* 59 (1972): 602-620.

Leffler, Melvin. "The Origins of Republican War Debt Policy, 1921-1923: A Case Study in the Applicability of the Open Door Interpretation." *Journal of American History* 59 (1972): 585-601.

Rhodes, Benjamin D. "Herbert Hoover and the War Debts, 1919-1933." *Prologue* 6 (1974):130-144.

NAVAL LIMITATIONS & DISARMAMENT

The London Naval Limitation Conference (1930) and the Disarmament Conference at Geneva (1932-1933) were the major events.

O'Connor, Raymond G. *Perilous Equilibrium: The United States and the London Disarmament Conference of 1930*. Lawrence: University of Kansas Press, 1962.